LEARNING

FROM THE

BEST

LEARNING

FROM THE

BEST

LESSONS FROM AWARD-WINNING SUPERINTENDENTS

SANDRA HARRIS

FOREWORD BY
DANIEL A. DOMENECH
EXECUTIVE DIRECTOR
AMERICAN ASSOCIATION OF SCHOOL ADMINISTRATORS

A JOINT PUBLICATION

CORWIN
A SAGE Company

AMERICAN ASSOCIATION
OF SCHOOL ADMINISTRATORS

Copyright © 2009 by Corwin

For information:

Corwin
A SAGE Company
2455 Teller Road
Thousand Oaks, California 91320
(800) 233-9936
Fax: (800) 417-2466
www.corwinpress.com

SAGE India Pvt. Ltd.
B 1/I 1 Mohan Cooperative
  Industrial Area
Mathura Road, New Delhi 110 044
India

SAGE Ltd.
1 Oliver's Yard
55 City Road
London EC1Y 1SP
United Kingdom

SAGE Asia-Pacific Pte. Ltd.
33 Pekin Street #02-01
Far East Square
Singapore 048763

Library of Congress Cataloging-in-Publication Data

Harris, Sandra, 1946-
Learning From the Best: lessons from award-winning superintendents/Sandra Harris.
    p. cm.
"A joint publication with the American Association of School Administrators."
Includes bibliographical references and index.
ISBN 978-1-4129-5983-4 (cloth)
ISBN 978-1-4129-5984-1 (pbk.)
    1. School superintendents—Handbooks, manuals, etc. I. American Association of School Administrators. II. Title.

LB2831.7.H37 2009
371.2′011—dc22   2008045088

09   10   11   12   13   10   9   8   7   6   5   4   3   2   1

Acquisitions Editor:	Arnis Burvikovs
Associate Editor:	Desirée A. Bartlett
Production and Copy Editor:	Jane Haenel
Typesetter:	C&M Digitals (P) Ltd.
Proofreader:	Marleis Roberts
Indexer:	Kirsten Kite
Cover and Graphic Designer:	Lisa Riley

Contents

Foreword

The American Association of School Administrators (AASA) is thrilled to partner with Sandra Harris and Corwin on *Learning From the Best: Lessons From Award-Winning Superintendents*. This important collection brings together the wisdom and expertise of our nation's top school system leaders into one volume.

Harris and her contributors take a practical look at how superintendents can address the leading challenges facing schools today. Their book illustrates how educational leaders can build relationships with diverse audiences—including parents, board members, community members, and the media—to help students succeed. It examines how superintendents can use collaboration and communication to build a sense of community in schools and the larger community, it offers guidance on how superintendents can manage the inevitable stresses of the job by becoming more resilient, and it outlines how superintendents can lead school reform efforts and have a positive affect on student achievement.

There is no official road map to success in the superintendency; however, by drawing valuable lessons from proven leaders, Harris has created the next best thing. Both new superintendents and veteran educational leaders will discover helpful insights in these pages. For those aspiring to be a superintendent, there is no time like the present to begin preparing for the job, and this book is a good place to start.

Many of the award-winning superintendents who contributed to this book have participated in AASA's Superintendent of the Year program. Since 1988, the Superintendent of the Year program has paid tribute to the talent and vision of the men and women who lead our nation's public schools. AASA has recognized and honored more than 1,000 public school leaders through the program over the past twenty-two years.

A common thread throughout the Superintendent of the Year program, and throughout this book, is a commitment to information sharing. I often remark that the superintendency is one of the most challenging positions in America today. It can also be a lonely position. When we bring together school system leaders to share their expertise and learn from each other, we foster success among our leaders, our schools, and, most importantly, the children we serve.

AASA is indebted to Sandra Harris for pulling together this important resource. We also owe a debt of gratitude to all the superintendents who have contributed so much to the Superintendent of the Year program over the last twenty-two years. Finally, I would like to thank Darlene Pierce, who has guided the Superintendent of the Year program since its inception. I invite you to learn more about the program and read our annual Superintendent of Year Forum white papers on the AASA Web site at www.aasa.org.

Daniel A. Domenech
Executive Director
American Association of School Administrators
Arlington, Virginia

Acknowledgments

Since 2005 I have completed two book projects with Corwin. One focused on award-winning elementary principals, and the second, on their counterparts at the secondary level. Both projects took seven to eight months to complete. When it was suggested that I do a best-practice book for superintendents, I knew this would be the hardest project to date. Principals are busy people, but superintendents are the busiest people of all. I began this project in spring 2007. It is now winter 2009, and the project has finally come to an end.

I would like to thank Arnis Burvikovs, my Corwin editor, for his encouragement. Thank you, also, to the individuals who reviewed this book. Their comments were insightful and very helpful. I want to especially acknowledge the work of Steven Murdock, a doctoral student and my graduate assistant at Lamar University, for helping me complete this project. A special thank you to all the incredibly busy individuals who are or have served as award-winning superintendents for sharing their best practices—Thank You!

PUBLISHER'S ACKNOWLEDGMENTS

Corwin gratefully acknowledges the contributions of the following individuals:

Ellen Bueschel
Professor of Educational
  Leadership
Miami University
Oxford, OH

Cathleen J. Chamberlain
Assistant Superintendent
Oswego City School District
Oswego, NY

Mike Ford
Superintendent
Phelps-Clifton Springs CSD
Clifton Springs, NY

David G. Hodgdon
Assistant Superintendent
Monadnock Regional School
  District
Swanzey, NH

Carol J. Lark
Superintendent
Douglas County School
  District
Minden, NV

Elizabeth J. Lolli
Superintendent
Monroe Local School District
Monroe, OH

Janie L. Nusser
Superintendent
South Seneca Central School
  District
Ovid, NY

About the Author

Sandra Harris is professor and director of the Center for Doctoral Studies in Educational Leadership at Lamar University in Beaumont, Texas, where she teaches classes in social justice and applied research and other administrator preparation courses. Formerly, she served as a teacher, principal, and superintendent in public and private schools. Her scholarship agenda includes administrator preparation, K–12 peer harassment, and building relationship-oriented, socially just school environments. She publishes and presents at regional, state, and national conferences on these topics.

Contributors

Brenda Dietrich
5928 SW 53rd Street
Topeka, KS 66610
Tel: (785) 339-4000
Fax: (785) 339-4025
dietrbre@usd437.net

Size of Student Population: 5,579 (2007–2008 school year)

Years as Superintendent: 13

Awards: 2007 Kansas Superintendent of the Year

2007 Finalist for National Superintendent of the Year

Web Site: www.usd437.net

George A. Goens
71 Litwin Road
Litchfield, CT 06759
Tel: (869) 567-1974; or cell: (860) 601-8100
gagoens@snet.net

Senior partner with Goens/Esparo, LLC (leadership and education consulting firm)

Years as Superintendent: 14

Award: Educator of the Year 1991, Wisconsin–ASCD

Web Site: www.georgegoens.com

James (Jim) L. Hager
Professor-in-Residence
Department of Educational Leadership
University of Nevada–Las Vegas

4505 Maryland Parkway, Box 45002
Las Vegas, NV 89154-3002
Tel: (702) 895-3602 (office)
jim.hager@unlv.edu (office)
traderjim41@embarqmail.com (home)

Size of Student Population: 62,000 K–12

Years as Superintendent: 20

Awards: National Superintendent of the Year 2004, Plato Corporation

NAACP Educators Award 2004, Reno/Sparks NAACP Chapter

National Superintendent of the Year Finalist, AASA, 2004

2004 Western Industrial Nevada, Reno, Nevada

Superintendent of the Year 2003, Nevada

Superintendent of the Year 2003, Nevada Association of School Boards

Saludos Hispanos, Educator of Distinction, one of Saludos Hispanos's 100 Educators of Distinction for the Year 2001

Cultural Awareness Award, Washington Education Association, 1998 Human Rights and Relations for the District's Diversity Plan

Superintendent of the Year of the Washoe County School District, Reno, Nevada

Web Site: http://education.unlv.edu/edl; www.hugehager.com

Pauline Hargrove
Little Cypress–Mauriceville Consolidated Independent School District
6586 FM 1130
Orange, TX 77632
phargrove@lcmcisd.org

Size of Student Population: 3,750

Years as Superintendent: 8
Olympic Torch Bearer (2002)
Oxford Round Table Representative (2003)

Awards: ATHENA Woman of the Year, Business and Professional Women's Association, 2004

Yellow Rose of Texas, Governor Rick Perry, 2005

Superintendent of the Year, ESC Region 5, 2006

Honor School Board, ESC Region 5, 2006

Educator Hall of Fame, Lamar University, 2006

Citizen of the Year, Greater Orange Area Chamber of Commerce, 2006

Paul Harris Fellow and Rotary President, Orange Rotary Club, 2006

Woman of the Year, Orange Altrusa Club, 2007

Person in the Spotlight, *Texas School Business,* April 2007

Web Site: www.lcmcisd.org

Chuck Holt

Lexington Independent School District

8731 N HWY 77

Lexington, TX 78947

Tel: (979) 773-2254

holtc@lexington.isd.tenet.edu

Size of Student Population: 1,005

Years as Superintendent: 8

Awards: 2004 Region VII Superintendent of the Year

2004, one of five state finalists for Texas Superintendent of the Year

Web Site: www.lexington.isd.tenet.edu

Gary Johnson

Superintendent

Skiatook Public Schools

355 S. Osage St.

Skiatook, OK 74070

Tel: (918) 381-9517

garyjohnson@skiatook.k12.ok.us

Size of Student Population: 2,737

Years as Superintendent: 17

Awards: Past President of Oklahoma Association of School Administrators

Past Chairman of Cooperative Council for Oklahoma School Administration

Special Merit Award for Leadership, Oklahoma Association of School Administrators

New multipurpose activity center named the Dr. Gary Johnson Activity Center by the Skiatook Board of Education

School District recognized as Member of the Year, Skiatook Chamber of Commerce

Web Site: www.skiatookschools.org

Mark Keen
Westfield Washington Schools
322 W. Main
Westfield, IN 46074
Tel: (317) 867-8010
keenm@wws.k12.in.us

Size of Student Population: 5,500, rapidly growing suburban district, Indianapolis area

Years as Superintendent: 11

Awards: Indiana Superintendent of the Year, 2006

AASA President's Technology Award

Civic Star Award

Citizen of the Year

Web Site: www.wws.k12.in.us

Paul Kinder
Blue Springs R-4 School District
1801 NW Vesper Street
Blue Springs, MO 64015
Tel: (816) 224-1300
pkinder@bssd.net

Size of Student Population: 14,000

Years as Superintendent: 11

Awards: Horace Mann Award, presented by Missouri NEA

Leadership for Learning Award, NASSP

2007 Missouri Superintendent of the Year

2006 Outstanding Board of Education of the Year, Missouri School Boards Association

2006 Best Places to Work Award, *Kansas City Business Journal*

Web Site: www.bluesprings-schools.net

Daniel King
601 E. Kelly
P.O. Box 1150
Pharr, TX 78577
Tel: (956) 702-5600
drking@psja.k12.tx.us

Currently Superintendent at Pharr-San Juan-Alamo ISD
Pharr, TX 78577

Size of Student Population: Over 30,000

Years as Superintendent: 9

Awards: Region I Superintendent of the Year 2006

Texas Superintendent of the Year 2006

Regional and State Bilingual Educator of the Year Awards

Inducted into the Hidalgo ISD Hall of Fame

Inducted into the Rio Grande Valley Walk of Fame

Hidalgo High School, one of best three high schools in Texas and one of best in the nation, 2006, National Center for Education Accountability

Hidalgo High School recognized as one of the best in Texas by Standard & Poor's

Web Sites: www.psja.k12.tx.us; www.hidalgo-isd.com

Brian Knutson
Community Unit School District 95
400 South Old Rand Road
Lake Zurich, IL 60047
Tel: (847) 540-4964
brian.knutson@lz95.org *or* bgkhawk@comcast.net

Size of Student Population: 6,500

Years as Superintendent: 15

Awards: 2006 and 2007, Academic Excellence Award for Charles Quentin School from Illinois State Board of Education

2006 Magnet Award, Lake Zurich Area Chamber of Commerce

2005 Gold Medal Award by *Expansion Management Magazine*, 14th Annual Education Quotient

2003 AASA Leadership and Learning Finalist

Web Site: www.lz95.org

Thomas Leahy
Quincy Public Schools (retired)
31298 375th Street
New Salem, IL 62357
Tel: (217) 833-2448
tfleahy@adams.net

Size of Student Population: 7,100

Years as Superintendent: 14

Awards: 2006 Illinois Superintendent of the Year

2007–2008 IASA President

Glenwood High School Hall of Fame Inductee, 2007

Western Illinois University Arnold Salisbury Ed. Admin. Leadership Award, 2005

Alliance Library System, Administrator of the Year, 2005

Web Site: www.qps.org

Thomas Little
Metropolitan School District of Perry Township
6548 Orinoco Avenue
Indianapolis, IN 46227
tlittle@msdpt.k12.in.us

Size of Student Population: 14,200

Years as Superintendent: 13

Awards: 2007 Ivy Technical Institute, Board of Directors

2006, Indiana Association of Public School Superintendents: District 3 Superintendent of the Year

2006, National School Boards Association, Technology District Salute Award

2005, Indiana Association of Public School Superintendents, Treasurer

2004, Indiana Secretarial Association Administrator of the Year

2003, Workforce Investment Board, Outstanding Service Award

2000 Community Alliance to Promote Advisory Board

Web Site: www.msdpt.k12.in.us

Tony J. Marchio
Appoquinimink School District
118 S. Sixth Street
Odessa, DE 19730
Tel: (302) 376-4101
tony.marchio@appo.k12.de.us

Size of Student Population: 8,300

Years as Superintendent: 15

Awards: Delaware Superintendent of the Year, 2003, 2006

Ten of the eleven schools in the district rated superior— one commendable

Test scores among the highest in Delaware

Web Site: http://apposchooldistrict.com

Michael McGill
The Scarsdale Public Schools
2 Brewster Road
Scarsdale, NY 10583
Tel: (914) 721-2410
mmcgill@scarsdaleschools.org

Size of Student Populationt: 4,593

Years as Superintendent: 23

Awards: 2007 New York State Superintendent of the Year

Web Site: www.scarsdaleschools.k12.ny.us

John Morton
Superintendent
Newton Public Schools USD 373
308 East First Street
Newton, KS 67114
Tel: (316) 284-6206
jmorton@newton.k12.ks.us

Size of Student Population: 3,750

Years as Superintendent: 11

Awards: E3: Educational Entrepreneurial Enterprise, a High School Charter Initiative 2006

Kansas Superintendent of the Year

2006 School News "Tech Savvy Superintendent"

2006 Intel & Scholastic School of Distinction Award, Chisholm Middle School, recognized as best secondary school in the nation for a collaboration and teamwork model that resulted in high student achievement

Walton 21st Century Rural Life Charter Elementary School

President-elect, Kansas Association School Administrators (2007–2008); President (2008–2009)

Standard & Poor's recognition of USD 373 as one of 21 of 296 Kansas school districts designated "Frontier Districts" with a perfect 100 percent rating in terms of efficiency of resources used to support teaching and learning

Web Site: www.newton.k12.ks.us

Robert E. Nicks
Center for Doctoral Studies in Educational Leadership
College of Education and Human Development
Lamar University
P.O. Box 10034
Beaumont, TX 77710

Tel: (409) 880-8676
Fax: (409) 880-7788
rnicks@sbcglobal.net

Size of Student Population: 21,000

Years as Superintendent: 9 (recently retired as Superintendent of Schools, Midland Independent School District, Midland, TX 79701)

Awards: 2003 Lamar University Educator Hall of Fame

2004 Regional Superintendent of the Year

2004 Texas Superintendent of the Year Finalist

2005 Texas A&M University Outstanding Educator Award

Web Site: www.MidlandISD.net

Current Web Site: http://dept.lamar.edu/leadership/FacultyStaff/Nicks/nicks.htm

Robert Olsen
Sturgis Public Schools
107 W. West Street
Sturgis, MI 49091
Tel: (269) 659-1501
rolsen@sturgisps.org

Size of Student Population: approximately 3,500

Years as Superintendent: 9

Awards: District has been recognized as an exemplary district

Governor's Award for Excellence, 2000

2006 Regional Superintendent of the Year, Michigan

2007 State Superintendent of the Year representing MASA

Web Site: www.sturgisps.org

Krista Parent
South Lane School District
455 Adams Ave.
Cottage Grove, OR 97424
Tel: (541) 942-3381, ext. 131
kparent@lane.k12.or.us

Size of Student Population: 3,000 in eleven schools, including two district-sponsored charter schools

Years as Superintendent: 8

Awards: 2007 National Superintendent of the Year

2007 Oregon Superintendent of the Year

2007 Young Alumni Award, University of Oregon

2007 Leading into Leadership Award

2007 Hometown Hero Award

2006 Educational Excellence Award

2006 Becky L. Sisley Award

Web Site: www.slane.k12.or.us

Jerry L. Patterson
Professor, Educational Leadership
University of Alabama at Birmingham
EB 212
901 13th Street South
Birmingham, AL 35294
Tel: (205) 975-5946
jpat@uab.edu

Size of Student Population: 12,000

Years as Superintendent: 7 (former superintendent of Appleton Area School District, Appleton, WI)

Awards: 1993, Recognized as one of top six school districts in the nation by *Expansion Management Magazine*, October

1992, Awarded Danforth grant to convene twenty-five of the nation's most visionary superintendents to develop key leadership principles for the twenty-first century

1992, Featured in *Executive Educator* magazine as one of the nation's outstanding superintendents

1991, Recognized as one of Wisconsin's Outstanding School Districts by Wisconsin Manufacturers and Commerce

1991, Selected by *Milwaukee Journal* in 1991 as one of Wisconsin's leaders for shaping the next decade

Web Site: www.ed.uab.edu/jerrypatterson

School District Web Site: www.aasd.k12.wi.us

Diane E. Reed
Associate Professor, Co-Director, Educational Leadership Program
St. John Fisher College
3690 East Avenue
Rochester, NY 14618
Tel: (585) 385-7257
dreed@sjfc.edu

Size of Student Population: 2,600

Years as Superintendent: 15 (retired in 2006 from superintendency of Honeoye Falls-Lima Central School District)

Awards: 2004–2006, Honeoye Falls-Lima Central School District recognized as a high performing/gap closing district by New York State Education Department

2005, Honeoye Falls-Lima Central School District named in top 1.6 percent of schools in nation by *Newsweek* magazine

2005, Honeoye Falls-Lima Central School District named in top 3 percent of schools in Upstate New York by "Business First"

2006, New York State Council of School Superintendents (NYSCOSS) Appreciation Award and President-elect

2005, New York State Association for Computers and Technology in Education (NYSCATE) Superintendent of Year Technology Award

School Address: Honeoye Falls, NY 14472

Web Site: www.sjfc.edu

School District Web Site: www.fhlcsd.org

Patrick Russo
Hampton City Schools
One Franklin Street
Hampton, VA 23669
Tel: (757) 727-2035
prusso@sbo.hampton.k12.va.us

Size of Student Population: 22,000

Years as Superintendent: 22 (schools in New York, Georgia, North Carolina, and Virginia)

Awards: 2008 National Civic Star Award, Virginia Community Visioning, Community Priorities Workshop

2007 Virginia Tech Excellence in Education Award, Community Priorities Workshop

2007 National Public Relations Association Golden Achievement Award, Schools Curb Appeal Initiative

2007 National School Boards Association Magna Award, In-Sync Partnership

2004 Sandhills RESA Superintendent of the Year

1996 Georgia Superintendent of the Year

1990, 1988, 1985 Executive Educators Top 100 Educators in America

Web Site: www.sbo.hampton.k12.va.us

Ronald D. Valenti
Blind Brook Public Schools
390 North Ridge Street
Rye Brook, NY 10573
Tel: (914) 937-3600
rvalenti@cnr.edu

Size of Student Population: 1,535

Years as Superintendent: 28

Awards: 2005 Distinguished Service Award, New York State Council of School Superintendents

Blind Brook-Rye UFSD included in *U.S. News and World*'s 100 Gold Medal High Schools, 2007

Blind Brook-Rye UFSD included in *Newsweek*'s top 100 high schools in America, 2005, 2006

2001 Excellence in Educational Leadership Award, University Council for Educational Administration

1986 Executive Educator 100: Selected as one of top 100 superintendents in U.S.

1979 Outstanding Educator: Selected by New York State Administrators' Association

Web Site: www.blindbrook.org

CHAPTER ONE

Introduction

There is no better place to be than where you are, and no better time than now to make a difference.

—Jim Kelly, member of the NFL Hall of Fame

The local school district, governed by community members and supported primarily through taxes, is a concept that originated in America more than 350 years ago. This unique pattern of providing education began in the Massachusetts Bay Colony in the mid-1600s and spread throughout the young colonies. During the Westward Movement, settlers formed small, isolated communities, and one of their first concerns was to build a school. The framers of the U.S. Constitution knew that if democracy was to survive, the masses must be educated. They did not, however, specifically mention education in the federal Constitution. Consequently, it is up to each state, through its constitution and statutes, to provide for the education of its citizenry, which has resulted in significant local control of the schools. And whose job is it to lead this critical effort on the local school district level? The superintendent, of course, is charged with this very challenging role of maximizing student learning.

ROLE OF THE SUPERINTENDENT

Houston (2006) notes that "the golden era for the superintendency lasted from the beginning until the middle of the 20th century, with a generation of community leaders who were respected for their business acumen and their moral courage in taking care of the nation's future through its common schools" (p. 2). Since the turbulence of the 1960s, the authority of the superintendent has lessened despite the increasing complexity of the superintendent's role. He or she is often subject to public criticism, for it is the superintendent who is the "face" of the school district and, as such, is charged with providing instructional leadership and with orchestrating the daily operations of one of the largest "businesses" in the community.

QUALIFICATIONS FOR THE SUPERINTENDENCY

Douglas Reeves (2004) described a qualified superintendent as a person who has managed an entrenched bureaucracy; who has developed a multimillion-dollar budget; who knows how to deal with a demanding community and an aggressive press; who has a mission, leadership skills, political smarts, and management prowess; who will improve teacher quality but is also an inspiring leader; and who is committed to the advancement of all children. He then noted that we want our leaders to be folk heroes who have the "insight of Lao-tzu, the courage of a New York firefighter, and the work ethic of Paul Bunyan" (p. 57). Additionally, the literature suggests that, to be successful, superintendents must understand instruction, know how to use data, be able to interpret accountability measures, provide resources, be visible, empower risk takers, encourage collaboration, lead diverse groups of stakeholders (Lashway, 2002), be devoted to students, have strong interpersonal skills, build community relationships (Cooper, Fusarelli, & Carella, 2000), and work with the school board (Dahlkemper, 2005). In short, the wisdom of Lao-Tzu, the courage of New York firefighters, and the work ethic of Paul Bunyan just might not be enough to do the job today!

PURPOSE OF THIS BOOK

As a former superintendent, I often felt overwhelmed and knew there was not enough time in the day to discover everything I needed to know and do to be most effective. Many times during the more than twelve-hour day (a typical workday for superintendents) when confronted with challenging issues, I would wonder what other superintendents would do in this situation. My purpose in writing this book, therefore, was to discover from award-winning superintendents what they feel has helped them successfully lead their schools. Over the past eighteen months, I have contacted over 100 superintendents who have been recognized for their effectiveness in leading students in their school districts to new levels of achievement. Twenty-two practicing and former superintendents responded by sharing some of their most effective practices. Collectively, these superintendents represent over 250 years of experience. Whereas many were selected to participate because they had been recognized for their professional leadership as superintendents, others were selected because their districts had been recognized for outstanding achievement during their tenures as superintendents. Some of the award-winning superintendents who participated in this project listed many of their recognitions; others listed only a few. They have led schools in sixteen states: Alabama, Connecticut, Delaware, Kansas, Illinois, Indiana, Massachusetts, Michigan, Missouri, Nevada, Oklahoma, Oregon, New York, Texas, Virginia, and Wisconsin. They have shared well over 100 good ideas for you to consider, revise, and implement.

I emailed award-winning superintendents inviting them to contribute to this book by detailing what they considered their best practices. My request was open-ended. I simply asked the superintendents to share those practices they considered to be most responsible for their effectiveness as leaders. After reading carefully through the submissions, I categorized the practices that were submitted into five primary areas based on the main theme of the articles' contents: Leadership That Transforms Schools, Community Building, Changing Times, School Reform, and a general advice section that I call More Creative Ideas That Work. There is much overlap in these themes as many submissions cover more than one topic area. In fact, leadership, community building, changing times, and school reform are so closely related that, in some cases, submissions actually discuss all of the topic areas. My rationale in placing submissions within a specific chapter was based on the following belief: *leadership* that transforms schools must be in place to *build community* within the schoolhouse and the larger community in these *changing times*, which are exacerbating the need for *school reform*. Edits were made in each submission, and I often divided longer submissions by topic area and placed them in different chapters. Using a fieldbook format, I attempted to keep the voice of the superintendents distinct and individual throughout the book; thus, the reader will notice a variety of writing styles.

At the end of each chapter (for chapters 2–5), I have included a brief summary of the research on that chapter topic and a summary of the award-winning practices superintendents shared with me. By glancing at the bulleted summary lists, the reader can quickly review the most effective practices included in that chapter. Reflection questions are included as well since learning about the most effective practices of others is important, but the real challenge is to take those ideas and revise and refine them to fit other school situations. The chapters conclude with a list of online resources to help readers gather extra information about supplemental ideas mentioned by the superintendents. Chapter 6 includes general advice, a recommended book list, and brief words of wisdom from the participating superintendents. Superintendents who responded to my query about their most effective practices represent an array of school districts with diverse populations, school sizes, and communities. The leaders are just as diverse in their experiences, yet all have been recognized many times for their strong, effective work as educational leaders.

Superintendents are not mythical heroes; instead, they are flesh and blood examples of heroes. I recently saw a sign that read something like, "If Celebrity were Integrity, . . . you would know our names." That sign could well have been about school superintendents. I have heard it said that a candle loses nothing when lighting another candle, instead, the room becomes brighter. So it is with sharing good ideas. We lose nothing by sharing; instead, the world is a better place when good ideas are shared, implemented, revised, and refined—over and over again.

CHAPTER TWO

Leadership That Transforms Schools

> *To know what to do is wisdom. To know how to do it is skill.*
>
> *To know when to do it is judgment. To strive to do it best is dedication.*
>
> *To do it for the benefit of others is compassion. To do it quietly is humility.*
>
> *To get the job done is achievement.*
>
> *To get others to do all of the above is leadership.*
>
> —Author unknown

Defining leadership is a challenge. Upon considering the etymology of the word *leadership*, Davies (2005) noted that it appears to be rooted in an Anglo-Saxon noun meaning *a course, way*, or *journey* and a verb meaning *to lead*. In other words, leadership has its source in the notion of one who leads the way or leads the journey. Bennis and Goldsmith (1997) said it especially well in the following:

> A leader is someone who has the capacity to create a compelling vision that takes people to a new place, and to translate that

vision into action. Leaders draw other people to them by enrolling them in their vision. What leaders do is inspire people, empower them. They pull rather than push. (p. 4)

With vision in mind, leaders focus on setting goals and inspiring and communicating the mission to others to make schools effective places for children. In this way, leadership is transformational. Leithwood and Jantzi (2005) identified three categories of transformational leadership practices in schools: setting direction, developing people, and redesigning the organization.

There is no doubt today that the primary goal and mission of schools is that of student achievement. Marzano, Waters, and McNulty (2005) conducted a meta-analysis of twenty-seven studies to investigate the influence of school district leaders on student achievement. These studies involved 2,817 districts and the achievement scores of over 3 million students. They identified five district-level leadership responsibilities that had a statistically significant correlation with average student academic achievement. The five responsibilities were collaborative goal-setting, nonnegotiable goals for achievement and instruction, board alignment and support of district goals, monitoring goals for achievement and instruction, and use of resources to support achievement and instructional goals.

The leadership responsibilities identified by Marzano and colleagues (2005) are consistent with Leithwood and Jantzi's notion of transformational leadership. Because the superintendent's responsibility is to provide the professional guidance and educational leadership needed to promote student success, his or her leadership duties include an array of tasks:

- Planning, operating, supervising, and evaluating programs, services, and facilities of the district
- Making recommendations regarding personnel selection
- Initiating the termination or suspension of employees
- Managing the day-to-day operations of the district
- Preparing and submitting a proposed budget
- Preparing recommendations for policies to be adopted by the board
- Overseeing the implementation of adopted policies
- Developing administrative regulations to implement policies
- Providing leadership for the attainment of student performance

- Organizing the district's central administration
- Performing other duties as assigned by the board of trustees

Of course, this list is just a beginning as the job responsibilities for superintendents have become increasingly complex over the years, a fact that underscores the importance of understanding that leadership does not happen in isolation. Instead, it is collaborative. As the quotation at the beginning of the chapter suggests, leadership incorporates the notion of being able to "get others to do . . ."

Because of the complex nature of the superintendency in today's world, there is a critical need for transformational leaders who can change schools into places where people effectively revise old ideas and practices into new ideas and practices (S. Harris, 2005c; Harris, Lowery-Moore, & Farrow, 2008). Southworth (2005) has noted that a critical element in changing a school's culture is an emphasis on continued learning characterized by collaboration, shared leadership, responsibility, and responsiveness to alternative ideas and approaches.

Houston (2006) argues that there has never before been a "greater need for leadership, advocacy, and activism from the super-intendent" (p. 3). Public education is the cornerstone of our democracy and by far the place where the majority of America's children are educated. Leaders must understand that what happens *in* the school is a reflection of what happens *outside* the school, within the larger community (Houston, 2006).

Effective superintendent leaders understand the nature of the districts they are leading, and they nurture the qualities of transformational leadership. As they implement leadership that emphasizes Marzano and colleagues' (2005) five responsibilities, they model the way. The award-winning superintendents who participated in this project are transformational leaders. Their effectiveness is evidenced in the submissions, which I have organized in this chapter by the underlying themes of setting direction, redesigning the organization, and developing people.

A basic leadership strategy for setting direction is shared by John Morton—a method using collaboration and communication. Robert Olsen discusses how to lead within the parameters of No Child Left Behind (NCLB). Patrick Russo describes a creative way to involve the community in setting direction for schools. Redesigning the organization is addressed by James L. Hager, who presents a strategy for identifying the district culture. Robert Olsen also addresses the notion of redesign as he shares district successes in creating "the absolute best conditions for learning." Another aspect of leadership that redesigns the organization occurs in the area of finances. Focusing on this topic, Ronald D. Valenti contributes information on how his district reorganized to reduce school district health care costs. Thomas Leahy, Gary Johnson, Robert Olsen, and Krista Parent suggest ideas for leadership that develop people. Collectively, these superintendents understand the importance of leaders who are committed to shared goals and who understand the importance of what superintendent Thomas Leahy calls "a daily recalibration of commitment to a vision."

Leadership Sets Direction by Communicating and Collaborating

John Morton
Newton, Kansas

Leading with communication and collaboration—these two practices can almost single-handedly make you a success or a failure as a superintendent. They are critical ingredients in administrative leadership at any level in today's schools and school districts.

Superintendents must model teamwork and collaboration at the top by working effectively in a very transparent way with the district-level and building-level teams. I have created a three-tiered system that appears to work well for our district. I meet weekly with the district office administrators (DOA) to deal with the major issues of the district. I meet biweekly with the district office team (DOT), which expands the DOA to include all levels of district operations. Finally, all building and district administrators meet the day following each board meeting to focus on issues of common concern and professional growth. A different administrator facilitates each meeting.

To build collaboration, treat everyone with equal respect. Bus drivers, secretaries, school nurses, teachers, aides, administrators—and everyone in between—deserve to be heard, appreciated, and respected. Most people equate direct, personal communication with respect. Collaboration needs to become embedded in a district's culture. It is part of our vision for excellence in USD 373 and is an important part of our activities at all levels of the district.

Remember, no matter how much you communicate, it never seems to be enough. Stay on message, but repeat it frequently and in a variety of ways until it becomes a part of the daily language of the school district. Practice *360-degree* communication; whether communicating up, down, across, or around, keep communication consistent and sustained. The benefits are immeasurable.

Leadership Sets Direction by Staying the Course

Robert Olsen
Sturgis, Michigan

First and foremost, regardless of what you may have heard and regardless of who captures the White House, NCLB is not going away. Education YES!—the state of Michigan's framework for school accountability—is not going away either. The reason? Ninety-five percent of these initiatives are appropriate for us now and well into the future. The details will change, but the essence of the initiatives will remain the same. Achievement and results are what it is now all about. Remember the directive from Covey (1992): *the main thing is to keep the main thing, the main thing!* As educators we are all proud when all our buildings receive very good passing grades and when all our buildings make AYP (Adequate Yearly Progress). But if we, for a moment, take our finger off the pulse of student achievement and fail to keep the main thing, the main thing—we *will* lose our momentum and struggle to stay on top of the learning game!

When we know we have the system moving in the right direction, it is the responsibility—actually, the duty and obligation—of every educator in the district to keep us moving in that direction. To make sure that everyone in the organization, from operational support staff to instructional support staff, from faculty to administration, lives up to that simple message is the primary goal of the district and the primary task that has to drive everything we do. Just as Jim Collins wrote in his book *Good to Great: Why Some Companies Make the Leap—and Others Don't* (2001), our challenge is relatively simple: identify appropriate direction, develop strategies that will help us move in that direction, and then measure whether or not we get there.

In our district, attention to the curriculum development process and our participation in the North Central Association's Commission on Accreditation and School Improvement (NCA CASI) process have provided the umbrella structure under which all our initiatives can be connected. The vision for the Sturgis Public Schools of the future must be the same as it has been for the past three years: that, given the choice, literally all children throughout this entire area—south-central Michigan and northeastern Indiana—would attempt to enroll in the Sturgis Public Schools. To reach that vision, we must hold ourselves accountable for creating high academic standards for all children. We must accept the scrutiny that the state and the public at large have foisted upon us with measurement standards like those already mentioned:

- No Child Left Behind legislation
- Education YES!
- The North Central Association system

We have learned how to work under this accountability microscope, and now we must learn to compete and excel under that microscope if we are to survive as an institution serving all kids from all kinds of backgrounds.

Our accomplishments have laid a foundation so that the Sturgis Public Schools can aggressively and strategically attack new goals and challenges constantly being faced, goals that get at the heart of our mission to improve student achievement and create a framework for accountability for every one of us in the organization. Our district has the beginnings of a professional learning community, but whether or not we fully evolve into one is up to each and every one of us. We have great things going on here, but we need to stay the course to realize our greatness for our students and for our community.

We know that the core mission of education is not simply to ensure that students are taught but to ensure that they learn. That simple shift—from a focus on teaching to a focus on learning—has been at the heart of NCLB, Education YES! NCA CASI, and the Sturgis Public Schools' instructional development plan for more than just a few years.

Three questions really have to drive everything we do:

- What do we want each student to learn?
- How will we know when each student has learned it?

- And, most importantly, how will we respond when a student experiences difficulty in learning?

We have devoted tremendous time and energy to designing the *intended* curriculum, and we have paid close attention these past few years to the *implemented* curriculum. Now we have to recognize that what really matters is the *attained* curriculum. What do students walk away with after we are done?

We all know that truly great schools and teachers judge their effectiveness on the basis of results attained, not on content covered. Dr. Ron Edmonds, the late great education researcher and reformer, challenged us several years ago when he emphasized that we can successfully teach all children. He reminded us that we already have the knowledge to do so. Whether or not we accept this challenge relies on how we feel about the fact that we have not done this so far. I only wish Dr. Edmonds could experience the kind of work that the people in this district do on a daily basis.

In Sturgis, we have all the ingredients for successfully helping *all students* achieve academic excellence:

- A community that provides the resources necessary to create the very best possible learning environments
- A school board that holds a common vision for the district, makes decisions based on what is best for all students, holds administrators/teachers accountable for student learning, and provides the best resources possible
- A superintendent who is committed to creating a sense of urgency surrounding academic excellence and who expects everyone in our district to share in that urgency
- Central office administrators and staff who are service oriented and focused on supporting teachers and principals in their quest for academic excellence with students
- Risk-taking principals who are constantly seeking to be strong instructional leaders and are striving to support teachers in their quest to become great
- A support staff committed to creating a positive learning environment
- Teachers who are confident, competent, and committed to ensuring that all students learn

By working together with a shared vision of the future, we achieve our goals, fulfill our mission, and reach our vision.

Leadership Sets Direction by Involving the Community in Visioning

Patrick Russo
Hampton, Virginia

Hampton is a built-out, landlocked, blue-collar, bedroom community. Demographics in the district are, however, quickly changing and include an older white population frequently disconnected from the majority, school-aged African American population.

Hampton City Schools (HCS) serves 22,500 students in thirty-six schools. Three years ago, only 57 percent of our schools made AYP. After deliberation, school division leaders decided that community ownership was the key to the creation of a high-performance school division within an aging, fiscally challenged community. With great hope and some anxiety, Hampton City Schools initiated the annual Community Priorities Workshop (CPW), first conducted in February 2005. This community engagement workshop has received national and state recognition, becoming the 2007 National Civic Star Award winner for Virginia and being presented with the Virginia Tech 2007 Excellence in Education Award.

The objective for the workshop was to engage the whole community in shaping a set of shared outcomes for the school division. A broad cross-section of critical community stakeholders was invited to ensure representation of students, parents, administrators, teachers, city council members, school board members, constitutional officers, city personnel, higher education institutions, neighborhoods, civic organizations, realtors, the military, business, and faith-based organizations.

In total, 140 individuals participated in the three-hour event. The crowd was divided into "like" groups who shared a similar frame of reference (for example, students met with students), and facilitators guided groups though a discussion that shaped goals. The whole group reconvened and reported. The large group was then divided into "mixed" groups to refine the goals. This process was intentionally designed so that all stakeholders could contribute as equals and become partners with Hampton City Schools, providing direction within the framework of Hampton City Schools' core mission of ensuring educational success for all students.

The workshop results were refined into six goals: recruitment, development, and retention of effective staff; facilities and technology development; parental involvement; building school and community partnerships; fashioning three- and four-year-old preschool and at-risk programs; and conducting a program audit. Subsequently, the school board took the bold step of adopting the results as division-wide community priority goals, and the superintendent turned them into action steps. Each central administration department and individual school was tasked with developing three to five simple, quantifiable, written objectives to support the community priorities, resulting in over 200 tools with which to implement them.

During the following school year, this work, supported with the spirited cooperation of a more fully engaged community, yielded amazing results.

- Teachers received a 14 percent raise over two years.
- The school board undertook a $400 million school construction project.
- 95.9 percent of community members stated that they understood the school division's mission and vision.
- Seven "One Church/One School" partnerships were created.
- The first three- and four-year-old preschool was started.
- An alternative education work team was initiated.
- The first program audit was completed.
- 79 percent of our schools made AYP, including all of our secondary schools.

There is no doubt that embracing all facets of the community in the process of defining the vision and focus of a school district is essential for a school district's success and support. This quality-driven process has allowed Hampton City Schools to realize gains some thought, at one time, unreachable. It is this process of community engagement that has allowed Hampton City Schools, as well as other school districts across the country, to engage all stakeholders in a manner proven to be of great assistance in gaining the support needed to change existing paradigms and improve student performance.

Leadership Redesigns the Organization by Identifying the Culture of the District

James L. Hager
Henderson, Nevada

Due diligence is the operative phrase when an individual is seeking or being sought to lead a school district, regardless of size. The school district's board of trustees solicits input from employees and community members about the skills, attributes, and experiences desired in their next superintendent. A headhunter is oftentimes employed by the board to assist in drawing up the profile of the "ideal" superintendent and then spends countless hours seeking candidates that meet the criteria of this desired individual. Once a cast of candidates is drawn and identified, scans of the candidates are conducted by community and business leaders, employee groups, or anyone who knows someone in a candidate's community, and, of course, the headhunter has thorough background searches conducted on each candidate. Now that the candidates are selected, the parade of champions begins. Each candidate is brought to town, presented to staff, community groups, parents, and business leaders, and ultimately interviewed by the board. At the conclusion of this process, a finalist is selected and typically screened one more time via a visit to her/his current place of employment. If all is well, a contract is tendered, negotiated, and finalized.

Given this process, you would think that the newly appointed superintendent would have a strong sense of the district's culture and the thinking of the various individuals and organizations comprising the school district community. Wrong! Most of the due diligence is centered on the superintendent candidate with little time allowed for the superintendent to have conversations with the district's many publics.

My technique for understanding the culture of a district to which I have just been appointed superintendent has always been contained in my written entry plan and includes the following elements:

1. I ask each principal to write me a one-page executive letter addressing the following five questions:
   - If I had children that could be enrolled in any school in the district, why should I enroll them in your school?
   - What are the top three strengths of the school district?
   - What are the three things I need to change in the district, in priority order?
   - What are the three things that I should not touch/change, and why?
   - What advice do you have for me?

2. I ask each central office administrator to write a one-page executive letter addressing the following five questions:
   - What is the one greatest strength of your department, and how does the department support student learning?
   - What are the top three strengths of the school district?
   - What are the three things I need to change in the district, in priority order?
   - What are the three things that I should not touch/change, and why?
   - What advice do you have for me?

3. I ask the leaders of each employee organization to write a one-page executive letter addressing the following five questions:
   - How would you describe the working relationship between the district and your association?
   - What are the top three strengths of the school district?
   - What are the three things I need to change in the district, in priority order?
   - What are the three things that I should not touch/change, and why?
   - What advice do you have for me?

4. Simultaneously, I schedule individual meetings with business, political, and community leaders to discuss their respective positions on the above five questions.

Once all this information has been received, I spend a considerable amount of time reviewing the information in an attempt to identify common strengths, weaknesses, issues, priorities, and sacred cows. In other words, I try to get a sense of the culture of the district. Following my review of the information, I place it in presentation format, then meet with each of the respective groups to discuss what I have learned and to seek any areas needing clarification or correction. Following these meetings, I use this information throughout my tenure to develop strategic initiatives for the district, as well as to serve as benchmarks on where we started together and the progression we have made to date.

By the way, this entire process is conducted and completed between the date of my appointment to the position and the date when I am officially scheduled to start the job.

Leadership Redesigns the Organization Through Instructional Leadership

Robert Olsen
Sturgis, Michigan

Early on in my career, it became abundantly clear that, collectively, our education establishment knows a great deal about teaching and learning. Additionally, academic and scientific researchers continue to churn out a treasure trove of research on learning, brain development, and instructional practice. Not long after that revelation, I came to understand that much of what we know through research and study will never get put into practice if there is the least bit of disconnect between that research and the practitioners' (teachers and administrators) past best practice, regardless of the depth and breadth of that research.

It has been my good fortune to have served as teacher and administrator in six different Michigan school districts representing the entire range of socioeconomic conditions. I understood early on that, regardless of what kind of preschool experiences children might have, the critical element in the learning process has to do with the relationship between teacher and child. The second most critical element in that process is the quality and depth of the teacher's preservice preparation and ongoing professional development once on the job. As such, we have decided that the most important thing we can do as an organization is to create the absolute best conditions for learning that we can while focusing on specific, targeted professional development outcomes for those most closely associated with the teaching and learning process (teachers, administrators, and related support staff).

In establishing a professional learning community, we in the Sturgis Public Schools have come to rely on research to define and guide our efforts. One very specific strand of research that has had a direct and lasting impact on our school district has virtually nothing to do with instruction, learning, or academic achievement; rather, it has everything to do with defining and establishing working relationships with all employee groups in our school community—relationships that will create the synergy necessary for optimal service to students.

"Getting to Yes" by Roger Fisher and William Ury from the Harvard Negotiations Project (1987), beyond providing a guide to effective interest-based bargaining and negotiations, has provided our district with a blueprint for defining effective communication focused on collaborative interaction and problem solving. Buying into the fundamentals spelled out in this project has allowed us to reach a win-win resolution to all major challenges facing our district over the past eight years, including finding a mutually acceptable plan to control costs associated with health care benefits. We are somehow able to solve the exact same problems over which other school districts seem to falter and stumble. Since adopting interest-based bargaining as our choice for negotiations, we have found that the model has transcended all organizational boundaries and become the operational guide for communication and interaction throughout the school community.

In respect to research impacting teaching and learning, I believe the works of Robert Marzano and Tom Guskey have had the most significant impact from an organizational perspective. Using much of their work in concert, we have narrowed our focus and have "ramped up" our professional development model to challenge and support our instructional staff (professional and support). We now have very specific, targeted, and ongoing professional development goals to ensure that all staff associated with the instructional process have the skills and tools necessary to enhance the achievement levels of all students throughout the district.

Rather than jumping each year to the "topic of the month" bandwagon, we maintain our professional development focus on the factors that have a direct impact on achievement. Here are but a few:

- A viable curriculum: using curriculum mapping, essential content, and extended-day learning programs
- Challenging goals and effective feedback: creating functional assessment plans, monitoring student achievement data, and revising our grading and reporting processes at every level
- Collegiality and professionalism: creating and nurturing our professional learning communities
- Parent and community involvement: extensive outreach and feedback opportunities are trademarks of our school district

Leadership Redefines the Organization by Reducing District Health Care Costs

Ronald D. Valenti
Rye Brook, New York

Educational leaders know that the major challenge confronting twenty-first-century policy makers is obtaining adequate financial resources to ensure increased student achievement and school performance. Two opposing forces inevitably threaten to collide: diminished revenue versus escalating expenditures.

Where do school leaders turn when growing taxpayer resistance and tightening economic conditions threaten to reduce local support and government aid? Increased public demands to lower class size, pressures to improve student performance on state-mandated tests, and the dramatic growth in remedial, second-language, and special needs populations demand higher school expenditures. If staggering cost increases were to stop at the academic gates of education, policy makers might enjoy a little breathing room; however, the appetite for increased expenditures expands well beyond instructional investments and outlays for student programs. Recent unprecedented soaring health care costs (averaging 10 percent annually since 2003), when coupled with the staggering employee retirement rate and energy expenses, are driving yearly budget hikes well beyond cost of living increases.

THE NEW YORK EXPERIENCE

The New York State experience in 2007 is well worth referencing. School district leaders throughout the state managed to keep the average tax levy increase to an incredibly low 3.9 percent, but only because then New York governor Eliot Spitzer and the state legislature were locked in a game of political one-upmanship that drove an unprecedented $1.7 billion into nearly 700 school districts throughout the state.

The big city school districts of Buffalo, Rochester, Syracuse, and Yonkers received double-digit revenue increases in 2007, whereas New York City garnered over $500 million in state aid and an extra $1.7 billion through a settlement from the Campaign for Fiscal Equity's lawsuit. An additional 112 high-need districts, struggling academically, received even more generous amounts of state monies through "Contracts for Excellence," which supplied funds to strengthen student and school performance. Principally due to this historic revenue infusion, 96 percent of New York budgets passed in 2007, which not only surpassed a prior record of 93 percent set in 2003 but also permitted some limited breathing room until the following year.

The question then, however, became, What will New York State do for an encore? State lawmakers immediately began warning that such dramatic revenue gains were unsustainable and suggested that school districts begin looking elsewhere to resolve the annual dilemma of developing balanced budgets that will warrant taxpayer approval.

WHERE SHOULD SCHOOL LEADERS TURN?

Nelson Rockefeller, governor of New York State from 1959 to 1973, once famously remarked, "Government is no fun when you have no money." Knowing that the revenue streams will remain, at best, modest and that alternative revenue sources (educational foundations, grants, gifts, school fees, etc.) will again be limited, policy makers have only one very unattractive option left—reduce expenditures.

Throughout history, school leaders have cut costs principally in noninstructional areas, such as in buildings/grounds maintenance and facilities upkeep. They have realized, however, that this well has run dry. In fact, the lack of attention and money for facilities improvement in many school districts over the past decade has led to a surge in capital construction projects and bond referenda to repair or replace the eroding infrastructures of our classrooms, science labs, facilities, and fields.

There is, then, only one place left to turn on the expenditure front, and that is toward the largest elephant in the room: personnel costs. Currently, between 65 and 80 percent of a school budget is spent on personnel expenditures, ranging from staff salaries to retirement and health insurance costs, and to social security, workmen's compensation, sick leave, personal leave, bereavement, and professional improvement activities (Brimley & Garfield, 2008). Many reasons explain why personnel expenses have eluded either the administrative scalpel or the management axe of budget cutters. First, education is a labor-intensive business, a human enterprise of the first order. We will always need qualified and certified teachers and support staff to serve our students' academic, personal, and social needs. Despite the huge gains in technology and some limited increases in virtual schooling (e.g., schools without classrooms, etc.), the essential design of our human enterprise will not change soon. As important, the competitive demands to recruit qualified and certified staff have been growing geometrically, particularly in the fields of math, science, and modern language instruction. Urban school districts, which are now shifting toward increased compensation and incentive plans for their teachers, are beginning to level the playing field with suburban school districts. Because the supply of qualified instructors is remaining constant (or, in some instances, declining) and the demand for teachers continues to increase, the market fundamentals requiring higher salaries and benefits for qualified educators obviously follow.

WHAT ALTERNATIVES DO SCHOOL OFFICIALS AND POLICY MAKERS HAVE?

In their attempts to balance quality schooling and recruitment in a competitive environment with the need to control costs, school officials and policy makers have two promising approaches, both of which this article will examine. First, the differential staffing model complements full-time teacher aides and teaching assistants with part-time teacher aides. The educational and supervisory benefits to students will be explained here, together with reduced structural costs, specifically for health care. Second, a partnership arrangement with professional staff will be examined that uses the collective bargaining model to negotiate equal sharing of health care increases (one of the fastest-growing components of school district budgets).

In both models—differential staffing and collective bargaining—the core emphasis is on reaching beyond short-term, cosmetic fiscal adjustments and institutionalizing more permanent, structural changes to reduce future health care costs to school districts.

DIFFERENTIAL STAFFING TO
REDUCE HEALTH CARE COSTS

Traditionally, Blind Brook-Rye, a 1,500-pupil, high-performing and high-wealth K–12 school district in New York State's suburban Westchester County, had been appointing full-time teacher aides when a student's academic, emotional, or behavioral needs warranted such according to the child's IEP (Individualized Educational Plan). This automatic, near-Pavlovian response from the district's Special Education Department was partly attributable to the department's unstable leadership (three directors were appointed within three years) and partly to enormous parental pressures, absent impartial hearing or legal action. Under siege, the district yielded to parental threats, with the number of full-time special education teacher aides ballooning to thirty staff members by the summer of 2003 and costing nearly $900,000 in salaries and benefits, which included full health care. In 2003, this expense alone accounted for nearly one-third of the $3 million special education budget, which represented about 12 percent of the entire school budget.

When I was appointed superintendent of schools in July 2003, we put in place, with school board approval, a short-term attrition plan to reduce full-time aides. This traditional cost-saving method of "reduction by attrition" was intended to minimize the political impact of a change in culture while we recruited new and more stable leadership for special education. By spring 2006, nearly three years later, the number of full-time aides was reduced by ten, which is a remarkable 33 percent reduction that saved well over $250,000 in salaries and health and benefit costs.

Although reduction by attrition worked modestly well, other educational forces were at work that forced a further assessment of the policy of recruiting only full-time teacher aides. First, a new, stable, and invigorated leadership of the Special Education Department determined that the instructional needs of students differed substantially from their behavioral needs and thus required a more differentiated staffing design. Second, the escalating mandate to provide safety and security in our post-9/11 environment, combined with a growing elementary enrollment, prompted requests for greater flexibility in supervising general and special education children, particularly during their morning arrivals, afternoon departures, and lunchtime/recess periods.

Both of these forces (differential staffing and flexible supervision), when viewed through the lens of fiscal stewardship, formed the foundation for a paradigm shift that began with the 2007–2008 school year. We thus moved from having only full-time teacher aides to a differential staffing model where teaching assistants complemented both full-time and part-time teacher aides, thus constituting an integrated services approach. Because the district's goals were both compelling and transparent, simply stated, children's interests trumped all others.

Differential staffing best serves students' instructional and behavioral requirements. Flexible supervision, delivered by part-time aides whose schedules are not regulated by confining contract regulations, best serves students' safety and security. The replacement of full-time teacher aides with part-time aides also made fiscal sense. First, it increased the productivity of each full-time equivalent position (FTE) by 30 percent due to the increase in the number of weekly work hours per position, which went from thirty hours (one full-time aide) to thirty-nine hours (two part-time aides). Therefore, two aides, each working nineteen and one-half hours per week, replaced one full-time, thirty-hour aide. By increasing the hourly pay rate for part-time aides to $20 per hour from the original $13 hourly compensation, a large, untapped pool of very qualified candidates emerged. Second, this restructuring also eliminated the health care costs of ten full-time positions, generating a net savings of more than $200,000 in the school budget, always of importance to taxpayers.

Although the interests of students remained primary throughout this change process (and continues to do so), additional benefits to students should not preclude taxpayer benefits. In fact, if there is an overriding twenty-first-century national imperative for school leaders and policy makers, it is precisely to formulate programs that enrich student learning while reducing the taxpayer burden.

Initial salary savings generated by replacing full-time with part-time positions was $71,000. More dramatic savings, $130,000, were realized in reduced benefits (health care, pension, etc.) generated by changing full- into part-time positions. Aggregate savings of $200,000 for a district with a $36 million budget is not inconsequential and represents nearly 10 percent of the year-to-year annual increase in the special education budget ($2.1 million) and almost 1 percent of the annual tax levy hike (5.4 percent).

In summary, the initial goals of the differential staffing model to strengthen program capacity, increase schoolwide supervision, and reduce costs were accomplished. The district will continue to evaluate the longer-term impact on program quality and fiscal stewardship.

COLLECTIVE BARGAINING TO REDUCE HEALTH CARE COSTS

Historically, business and industry led the way in inaugurating employee benefits such as retirement plans, sick leave, and insurance coverage. It was not until 1950 that public education, due to the low wages generally paid to teachers, began to supplement salaries with various fringe benefits. Because these benefits were eventually tax free, and along with good working conditions and improving salaries, they increased job satisfaction and became motivators of efficiency and heightened productivity (Brimley & Garfield, 2008).

In the past decade, however, the costs of social security, pension contributions, and medical insurance have increased significantly. Since 2003, the health premium costs of Blue Cross–Blue Shield, a major health provider for government employees, have surged 48 percent. In other words, a family plan that was $9,737 in 2003 is currently $14,379. Social security contributions, as of 2007, for a salary level of up to $97,500 were 15.3 percent of the salary (7.65 percent paid by the employer, 7.65 percent, by the employee). This overall escalation in benefit costs has now shifted the entire collective bargaining process away from salary discussion to a negotiation of benefits.

Since school districts have no control over certain benefits, such as social security, and only limited control over pension and retiree expenses, the negotiating field has focused on health insurance, which is now the *new* 800-pound elephant in the room. Initially, most districts paid 100 percent of all employee health premium expenses. Over time, however, school officials gained a small foothold by demanding limited dollar contributions from each employee and eventually negotiating percentage contributions toward premium costs. A review of percentage contributions throughout Westchester and

Rockland counties, located in New York State, revealed that, of the fifty-five school districts reporting, forty-five required employees to make a percentage or dollar contribution. Of those that negotiated a percentage, the contribution ranged from 5 to 15 percent of the premium costs.

With burgeoning increases in health premium expenses, however, even this incremental approach has proved inadequate. In negotiations with the Blind Brook-Rye Teacher's Federation, the school board determined that a more dramatic approach was needed, specifically, insisting that all future premium increases be shared equally by the teachers and the school district.

The board's plan was simple: freeze the current percentage contribution at 11.5 percent of the 2007 premium. For a family plan, the teacher's contribution was $1,693 (11.5 percent × $14,722). Any additional costs over the duration of the four-year agreement would be equally borne by the school district and teacher. Using the assumption that the average annual increase is 10 percent, a teacher's rate of contribution would escalate proportionally. For example, if the family plan premium in New York did increase by 40 percent—from $14,722 in 2007 to $20,610 in 2011—teachers would shoulder 50 percent of the annual increase beginning in 2008. In other words, they would pay over that period the annual base premium of $1,693 in addition to one-half of the increase each year (although for the 2007 school year, teachers only paid 30 percent of the annual increase in addition to the $1,693 base premium). Based on this partnership formula, the district's contribution to health insurance ended up being considerably lower over the four-year period.

Both approaches—differential staffing, which reduces the number of employees receiving full-time benefits, and collective bargaining, which increases the employee's share of health care costs—promise to help districts control costs while maintaining solid education for our students.

Leadership Develops People Through Servant Leadership

Thomas Leahy
New Salem, Illinois

This superintendent's solution to being an effective leader is to keep in mind students, staff, and community—with the main focus on the *students*. The turning point and beginning for me was the desire to be a superintendent.

Rodger Hannel, a colleague and longtime friend, helped me understand the impact, influence, and authority that a superintendent carries. During the flood of 1993, West Pike Unit 2 battled the Mississippi by defending an elementary building in Hull, Illinois, with volunteers and thousands of sandbags. Rodger and I, along with twenty volunteers, wound up on the roof at midnight (the magic time to collect the $212,000 insurance claim). There was one life jacket and one can of bug spray. Rodger had both of them, and I knew then that, as superintendent, he had authority.

Seriously, though, the superintendent has the responsibility, authority, and burden to influence others in a positive way. We learn what to do and what not to do from those around us. I learned "what to do" from Rodger as a mode of operation, and I thank him for that. I have continued to reinforce and expand on that manner of operation with the great central office team at Quincy Public Schools. That mode of operation is service to students, staff, and community. Staying focused is key.

I have heard that landing on an aircraft carrier is like putting a postage stamp on the floor and jumping off a couch head first to lick it. Being a superintendent in today's climate is equally challenging, if not more so. We experience numerous external forces. With that being said, we must be of service, along with and in spite of external forces—including laws and mandates. Service must continue in spite of the pressures. I have found that through *trust*, one can work wonders. I learned about trust from my father, Francis C. Leahy. He was very clear in his expectations about telling the truth. He once told me that he would always support me unless he learned that I had not been truthful. The thought of disappointing him has stayed with me every day of my life. A great foundation was formed within my family.

In the book *The Servant Leader* (2003), Ken Blanchard and Phil Hodges remind us that we must lead with our heart, our head, our hands, and our habits. Leading with the heart emphasizes being a servant leader rather than a self-serving leader and stresses successor-ship, which is leaving the world better than we found it. Service through the heart may be threatened if we don't assess the situation by identifying what is or is not at risk. If the danger is not real and only imagined, we will spend time and energy for no reason. Applying trust, faith, hope, and love may be our best actions. The leadership vision must be centered on doing the right thing. Our capacity for change will drive our ability to lead with our hands.

Three years ago, we (Quincy Public Schools) looked at district reorganization. We asked a simple question of third-grade parents about changing K–3 schools to K–5 schools. Parents responded with an overwhelming "yes." I said, "Let's go." When I looked around, however, no one was behind me. Why? The people in my district were at different levels of change capacity. A responsibility of the superintendent is to prepare the school community for change and then to provide support for implementation. A daily recalibration of commitment to a vision, encouragement and feedback, truth and continual growth will affect leading with our habits. Daily recalibration of the commitment to a vision includes encouragement and feedback and finding truth tellers who will give you the straight of it.

I have had individuals say, "I wouldn't have your job"—I am happy about that. However, others say, "I'm gonna have your job!"—I am not so happy about that! It is a challenge to stay focused with your eye on the ball when you are under fire. In my first year at Quincy, I was initiated by the media. It was exciting at first. There were articles in the newspaper; I was on TV and radio. Then came letters to the editor critical of Quincy Public Schools and of me, and these asked for my resignation. One such letter arrived within my first year as superintendent at Quincy. My younger brother, Jim, had been sending news articles to our ninety-five-year-old mother, Elizabeth Burtle Leahy, in Denver, Colorado. Upon receipt of this letter, Mom phoned me on my cell phone. She said, "Are you OK?" And of course I answered yes. She referred to the letter and wanted to know if the guy who wrote it was a board member. I answered, no. She persisted by asking several times if I was OK and if she could be of help. I continued to respond that all was well and not to worry. She then said, "Where does he live?!!" Now with that, she was coming to the rescue. I smiled, thanked her, and said all is fine. Part of me wanted to help her find this individual, for I knew from experience that she could dish out the necessary attitude adjustment.

Fortunately, and for the most part, I have learned and adjusted to the media. It is difficult to sit down at the peace table when bullets are flying overhead. The key is *stability*, the kind of stability found through service. We experience emotion and passion when dealing with parents and grandparents, and now, being one (a grandparent), I understand that passion. Joyce and I have three children and eight grandchildren. The entire family is such a joy and support system for me. But now with grandchildren, "it is serious." When those around us are unstable, superintendents need to remain calm and collected, for we may be the only stabilizing factor in the room.

However, there are times when you have to stand your ground, especially when we have identified the tough issues and must work to fix the problems. We know that boards of education are a unique group. Individuals can enter a room, and when combined with others, a new life forms. We also know that individual board members by themselves are not in a position of authority unless we allow it. They are a collective authority when they are at a convened meeting, whether in attendance by phone or with their feet under the table. Some of my greatest challenges, met either through maintaining stability or standing my ground, have come when directing and redirecting the board, especially when I had a board member tell me they wanted special treatment. I am reminded of the high school basketball regional games. A board member cut into the ticket line and wanted special treatment. I redirected him by politely stating that he needed to wait his turn. He responded, "I'm your boss." I quickly responded with, "You are one of seven; the entire board together is my boss."

It is of utmost importance for superintendents to develop personal and professional mission statements. These should include goals, values in rank order, the importance of identifying the truth tellers, a plan for keeping a journal and daily living manual, concentration on solitude and prayer, rest and exercise habits, and a set of memorized emergency numbers. A servant heart begins with a vision.

In conclusion, let's keep our position in life in perspective. I do this with a final story. Some years ago when I was in my first superintendent's position at Payson, Illinois, I was walking through the student cafeteria at the K–3 lunch time. A young second grader asked the lunch supervisor who I was. She explained that I was the boss over everyone. He responded, "How about Jesus?"

Finally, we will move forward together utilizing our heart, head, hands, and habits. *I am your servant.*

Leadership Develops People
Through the Power of Collaboration

Robert Olsen
Sturgis, Michigan

Virtually all of the successes the Sturgis Public Schools has realized as an organization over the past nine years are a direct result of the power of collaboration—the power of "we." From projects, such as passing a bond in 2000, to controlling insurance costs, to negotiating contracts without the usual rancor, nothing would have been accomplished without a commitment to solving problems collaboratively. The essence of leadership is collaborative; it is about establishing relationships, then managing those relationships through the practice of key principles: trust, passion, courage, the common good, a focus on performance, and keeping it real.

- Trust: Maintaining a trusting relationship ensures a solid, productive working culture. When that trust is broken, everyone in the district pays for it for years to come.
- Passion: Passion is an essential motivating force because there is no substitute large enough to move us to do the great things we do for kids every day.
- Courage: Courage requires trusting in and empowering others. It takes courage to ask the tough questions while giving the difficult answers. It takes courage to find win-win solutions to the day-to-day problems.
- The common good: Balancing the needs of all stakeholders is an almost impossible task, yet the honest attempt to do things for the common good reaps benefits far beyond what the latest and greatest strategic plan might promise.
- Focus on performance: Over the past few years, we have learned how the power of focus and the results it yields has the capacity to transform a school. We must ask and answer the "So what?" question with every practice and every program in our district.
- Keeping it real: Being honest and forthright even when it might appear to be to your disadvantage is about being real. This is what it means to define oneself as a real person and a real leader.

Through good and bad experiences, I have learned to appreciate the impact that a grassroots, collaborative leadership style has on what school districts desire most: getting good results. Through these lessons, I have learned how the power of "we" rather than the genius of "me" has a multiplier effect on the human capital of a school district. Finally, I have seen this power allow our district to be in the best possible position to do the right thing, at the right time, and, always, for the right reasons.

Leadership Develops People Through Implementing Book Clubs

Krista Parent
Cottage Grove, Oregon

After I took on the role of superintendent, I began to ask myself questions about how our leadership team was spending its time together. Typically, all principals, assistant principals, supervisors, and central office administrators met twice a month for meetings. These meetings lasted approximately three hours and dealt with lengthy agendas—sometimes twelve to fifteen items. The items on the agenda were the typical suspects, mostly related to budgets, personnel, and operational matters. After about thirty minutes, administrators assumed a "glazed" look and often hurried out of the meetings to get back to their real work. I quickly began to question this use of time and assembled my central office team to discuss why we were meeting in this way and what they would think about a major change. The central office administrative team jumped at the chance to do something different.

My original pitch was that we should be spending the majority of our time together focusing on our core mission—teaching and learning—and that the other facets should take a backseat. I thought a good starting point for our administrative leadership team would be to read a book together and discuss the ideas from the book in relationship to what we were currently doing in our district. This meant I needed to do some reading to identify the perfect book to start us off. I knew that, if I didn't set this up correctly, it could undermine the whole strategic change. I quickly settled on two books—*Whatever It Takes* by DuFour, DuFour, Eaker, and Karhanek

(2004) and *Transforming Schools* by Zmuda, Kuklis, and Kline (2004). I asked my central office team to read both books so we could begin planning how to structure our book conversations with the administrative leadership team. We spent nine months reading the two books (several chapters at a time) and discussing them at our twice monthly administrative leadership team meetings. The three district administrators and I took turns facilitating these conversations. We identified several instructional strategies and critical friends' protocols (structures that encourage safe exchanges of ideas) to teach our leadership team, and we used these as we facilitated the book conversations.

We utilized two self-assessment tools with the leadership team to identify the areas we needed to nurture. The two self-assessment tools included Tim Waters's 21 Areas of Leadership Responsibility and the Children's Literacy Initiative Blueprint—*A Blueprint for Literacy Leadership*. Interestingly, there were three common areas identified from each self-assessment tool important to all leadership team members. From the 21 Areas of Leadership Responsibility, administrators identified Intellectual Stimulation; Knowledge of Curriculum, Instruction, and Assessment; and Change Agent as the three priority areas for development. From *A Blueprint for Literacy Leadership*, administrators identified Craft Leaders, Thinkers, and Practitioners; Children's Literature; and Special Interventions as the three main areas of needed growth.

Our transformation from a team of administrators to a true learning community team can be traced back to this bold move, which dramatically changed the way we had always done business. We have continued with our administrative leadership team book clubs to the present and have expanded the book club concept to include the whole school district, including the school board. We have plans to someday expand the book club out into the community. For now, the book club concept has been our major tool for professional development across the district. It is a fairly inexpensive tool that yields significant benefits and is not a "one-shot" professional development model. The book club conversations continue long after the book is read, and new books get compared to previously read books. The books are always available to reread at your own leisure, which accommodates everyone's learning style and needs.

Described below are three other ways we have moved the book club concept beyond the administrative leadership team.

Book Clubs for Credit

To expand our circle of reading to include instructional staff, we decided to offer a variety of book clubs throughout the year that staff members could participate in for credit. These book clubs occurred after hours, three times each term, with assignments given between sessions. The book clubs were facilitated by one of the four central office administrators. The book clubs were organized around specific themes, with an emphasis on teaching participants effective literacy-based instructional strategies. Some of the book clubs for credit included Children's Literature, Building Background Knowledge, Strategies That Work, Effective Writing Strategies, and Blogs, Wikis and Other Technology Tools.

For example, in the Children's Literature Book Club, participants read a variety of awarding-winning children and young adolescent novels. During the book club sessions, instructional strategies for the classroom would be modeled for use with the novels. Assignments included scheduling a central office administrator (including the superintendent) to observe in the classroom when a new strategy was being implemented. In addition to lively discussions about the books, participants were asked to journal their responses to a number of prompts focused on the reading. Book surveys were developed to explore the interests of their students. The book surveys were shared across the book club and across grade levels, for example, kindergarten teachers shared their book surveys with high school English teachers.

In the Effective Writing Strategies Book Club, participants read four books—*Because Writing Matters* (National Writing Project & Nagin, 2006), *Teaching Adolescent Writers* (Gallagher, 2006), *Writing Next* (Graham & Perin, 2007), and *Boy Writers* (Fletcher, 2006). During each session, the book club facilitator employed a variety of protocols and strategies to engage participants in deep conversations about how writing should be taught. Participants discussed concepts and strategies and chose ideas to implement in their classrooms. The writing book club also developed recommendations for furthering the district's writing plan.

The book clubs for credit are beginning their third year. Over half of the instructional staff in the district has taken at least one book club. We are now working to expand the book clubs to include more staff, not just central office administrators.

WHOLE DISTRICT BOOK CLUBS

In the spring of 2006, we decided to take our book club concept to the whole district staff to boost our K–12 literacy efforts. Our district administrative team had read approximately forty books on literacy over the course of eighteen months. We asked all principals and assistant principals to choose one of the forty books and to give a book talk to the entire administrative leadership team. This was a quick way to get the same level of knowledge out to the whole team, and we desperately wanted to get the information to all the instructional staff. Then we narrowed the book list down to our top twenty reads and went on a school tour giving a brief book description of each of the twenty books. Next, we "went out on a limb." We asked *all* teachers, specialists, librarians, technology staff, and educational assistants to choose one of the twenty books to read over the summer and to come back in August prepared to share their learning with colleagues from around the district that read the same book.

Our next step was to ask for twenty volunteers to be prepared to facilitate the book club discussions when staff returned in August. The facilitators included myself, central office administrators, principals, librarians, reading specialists, the family resource center director, and classroom teachers. This activity replaced the typical district "welcome back" wherein 250 staff members assemble in straight rows listening to a series of talking heads share their goals for the upcoming year. The activity went off without a hitch, and we received rave comments from a number of staff members. All staff members left their first book club meeting with a plan for how to implement their new strategies into their classrooms in the fall. A follow-up book club for these groups was scheduled for three months later to share their ideas after they had had time to implement some of their new learning.

For the summer of 2007, all instructional staff read the same book, and our plan was to bring the author of the book to our district book club in August (2007) to facilitate the next phase of conversations focused on writing.

SCHOOL BOARD/LEADERSHIP BOOK CLUBS

As a zealous first-year superintendent in 2001, I attempted to pull off a book club with my new school board. I started first by assigning them an article to read in preparation for our annual summer board work session. This turned out to be only moderately successful, mainly because I had very little experience in this area and I didn't do a good job setting up the activity. The following summer, I assigned them a book to read over the summer, thinking that the method had been so successful with my administrative leadership team that it would also help get the school board focused on the right things. For those board members who actually read the book, we made some progress, but I still only rated the activity as moderately successful.

I had follow-up, private conversations with a few of the board members to explore whether this strategy could be an effective one with the school board. What I found out from listening to their feedback was that even the most experienced board members were a little reluctant to move into the teaching and learning conversations because "they weren't the experts in that area." This was a good lesson for me, and I backed off the book club format with the school board for the next several years and focused more on sharing how the book clubs were being used with the staff and the effect this strategy was having on our work.

During the summer of 2007, I came back to the book club format with the school board, but I combined it with the book clubs we were doing with our entire administrative leadership team. I believed that the culture in the district had changed significantly since that first year in 2001, and, in fact, our school board appeared to be fully on board with our summer books clubs.

SUMMARY COMMENTS

The book club concept has been a powerful tool for moving our district through a series of transformations that have led to significant increases in student achievement. Our high school students have gone from being significantly below the state average on the Oregon Statewide Assessments to significantly above the state average and are among the best in a high-performing county. Suggestions for new reads are now coming in from across the district. No longer am I the sole provider of books for the book clubs. This strategy has been effective for getting information to all staff members in a relatively quick and fun manner. Of all the modes we've used for professional development, this one has had the greatest impact across all levels of the district. It has also helped establish a culture focused on our core mission—learning. Our early reading focused on K–12 literacy, and recently our reading has moving into thinking about the future. Our school board and administration are truly unified around our work, and the book clubs have been a catalyst for this collaboration.

Leadership That Develops People Is Important

Gary Johnson
Skiatook, Oklahoma

Leadership serves as the foundation for successful superintendent/ school board relations and school improvement. To set a tone of excellence in a school district, you must begin with the example set at the top. This example is set by the superintendent and school board and is filtered through the leaders at each site.

You must approach those leaders around you with the attitude that everyone is going to settle for nothing less than being #1 in every aspect of school business. I begin each year with a statement to my leadership cabinet that goes something like, "although you should always have a plan for your site and for your program, you must have a plan for your life first because you must strive to be excellent in your life's journey if you expect excellence from your staff and students."

I created the Skiatook Leadership Institute in 2006. This is a one-day professional development opportunity for leaders that we host in August to prepare for the beginning of the school year. It is a time to motivate and inspire our leaders from across the district. We bring in guest speakers who have exhibited great leadership traits in their life and business. We also utilize some of our own personnel who exemplify exceptional leadership qualities. Our motto for this institute is, "Setting the standards that others follow." Here is the schedule for a recent Skiatook Public Schools Leadership Institute:

8:30–9:00	Breakfast
9:00–9:05	Welcome—Dr. Gary Johnson
9:05–9:50	Steve Cantrell—Principal, Newman Middle School, "Leadership: Explore the Possibilities"

9:50–10:00   Break

10:00–11:00   Dr. Tom Agnew—Professor, Oral Roberts University, "How to Thrive as a Teacher Leader"

11:00–12:00   Dr. Jim Myers—Professor, Oral Roberts University, "Teacher Leaders: Why? What? How?"

12:00–12:30   Lunch

12:30–1:15   G. T. Moody—Campus Minister, Life Church, Stillwater, Oklahoma, "Core Leadership"

1:15–2:00   Dr. Gary Johnson—Superintendent, Skiatook Public Schools, "Leadership Style"

2:00–2:10   Break

2:10–3:10   Rick Brinkley—President of Tulsa Area Better Business Bureau, "What to Do When You Are Ready to Throw in the Towel"

3:10–3:15   Conference Evaluation

Leadership sets the foundation for everything that can or will happen, good or bad, in a school district. Success and failure truly starts at the top of the pyramid, with the superintendent and school board relationship. Their relationship begins or ends with the question of compatibility. My dissertation study was based on the importance of compatible relationships among superintendent, school board, and community power structure and the effect this relationship has on student achievement. The study proved to be very informative and beneficial with regards to the correlation between relationships and student achievement. The data demonstrated that a compatible relationship correlated with a higher-achieving school district and, conversely, an incompatible relationship correlated with a lower-achieving school district.

I truly believe that the work I am doing in helping people understand the importance of matching leadership styles with board types is crucial in improving student achievement across the country. It is obvious that the importance we have placed on leadership from the top down in Skiatook has made a difference in our school system as well as in our community.

SUMMARY

Leadership Research

Set direction, develop people, redesign the organization, promote student learning, collaborate on goal-setting, implement non-negotiable goals for achievement and instruction, emphasize board alignment and support of district goals, monitor goals for achievement and instruction, and dedicate resources to support achievement and instructional goals, advocacy, and activism.

Best Practice Ideas for
Leadership That Transforms Schools

- Stay the course
- Involve the community in visioning
- Promote the vision
- Identify the district culture
- Be an instructional leader
- Align activities with shared goals
- Hire/retain those who support the shared goals
- Serve those in the district
- Engage everyone in the district in continued learning
- Lead by example
- Be collaborative
- Provide time for learning
- Use resources creatively
- Remember, education is not about teaching—it is about learning

LEADERSHIP REFLECTION

1. What does your leadership look like?

2. In what ways are you a transformational leader?

3. In what ways does your leadership emphasize goal-setting and commitment to those goals?

4. In what ways does your leadership redesign the organization for improved student achievement?

5. In what ways does your leadership develop people to become stronger leaders?

6. Where are you weak in these areas?

7. Write a prescription for improvement in making you a more transformational leader.

8. What ideas in this chapter were the most important for your school district?

9. How can you implement or revise ideas in this chapter to improve your district?

ADDITIONAL RESOURCES

Children's Literacy Initiative. (2000). *A blueprint for literacy leadership.* Retrieved March 26, 2008, from http://www.cliontheweb.org/principals_blueprint.html

Education YES! A yardstick for excellent schools. http://www.michigan.gov/documents/Final_Revised_Ed_Yes!_50938_7.pdf

Harvard Negotiation Project. http://pon.harvard.edu/hnp

North Central Association, Commission on Accreditation and School Improvement. http://www.ncacasi.org

21 Areas of Leadership Responsibility. Retrieved May 24, 2008, from http://www.nwrel.org/request/2005nov/appendixa.html

CHAPTER THREE

Community Building

When the best leader's work is done the people say, "We did it ourselves."

—Lao-Tzu

uilding community in a school and its surrounding area means that all levels, from students, parents, and school personnel to local businesses and neighborhoods, unite to support local schools. This does not just happen accidentally; instead, respectful communities are built by design and fostered to grow under superintendent leadership.

Before superintendents can build strong foundations within the larger community, they must first build community within the school district itself, which includes the school board as well as each campus at the building level. One way to do so is to establish collaborative learning environments, often termed Professional Learning Communities (PLCs), at every level of the school community. Fullan (2001) identified shared vision and purpose as essential to implementing and sustaining PLCs. He emphasized the importance of direction and leadership for them to function wisely and warned that they cannot be left to function serendipitously; the superintendent must ensure that this shared vision and purpose are in place. Thus, DuFour (2004) identified three principles that must become deeply embedded in school cultures to sustain the PLC model: ensuring that students learn, creating a culture of collaboration, and improving academic achievement. These principles are in keeping with the Leithwood and Jantzi (2005) description of transformational leadership that sets direction, restructures the organization, and develops people.

The foundation for building a sense of community in schools and in the larger community is trust. Covey (2006) wrote that building trust is a function of both character and competence. While character is about integrity and credibility, competence demonstrates to those around us that we are capable of getting the job done well. Communication is the vehicle that transmits our level of competence to others. Hoy and Miskel (2005) argue that communication permeates every aspect of school life and consumes the majority of a leader's time. They recommend that superintendents strengthen communication resources by refining their sending, listening, and feedback skills. To enhance sending skills, avoid educational jargon, provide clear, complete information to listeners, hold conversations away from noisy, busy environments, use multiple media sources, and communicate face-to-face when conveying complex messages. Superintendents with strong listening skills are active listeners, attentive, question for improved understanding, encourage, paraphrase, notice the feelings of others, and summarize. Superintendents with good communication skills ask questions, describe behavior, paraphrase what the speaker has said, and are observant of nonverbal forms of communication.

Building PLCs requires superintendents to be collaborative in setting goals, working with school boards, designing leadership teams at the district and school level, and involving the larger community. When involving external partnerships, Pawlas (2005) identified ten components of a well-developed school-community plan to guide leaders. These include:

- providing the community with school information,
- providing the school with community information,
- nurturing and sustaining public confidence in the schools,
- securing support from the community for area schools,
- developing a common purpose and goals for achievement,
- developing community understanding of the importance of education to the community's economics and social life,
- keeping the community informed of new education trends,
- developing an atmosphere of cooperation between the school and other community agencies,
- gathering evaluative information from the community about the school district's educational needs, and
- building public goodwill toward the school.

Efforts to build community must include every level, from the school board to individual campuses to the larger community, as all individuals work together in support of the school. With this in mind, I have organized the submissions that follow to begin with uniting the school board, then with developing community at the district/campus level, and, finally, with building the larger community. John Morton and Chuck Holt describe strategies that guide their work in building community with the board. Next, Robert Olsen emphasizes the importance of everyone in the district in developing people. Offering suggestions to develop community at the district/campus level, Brian Knutson discusses building a PLC in his district, and Thomas Little suggests three key components needed for this to happen. Paul Kinder shares how his district has built community through collaboration and communication. Brenda Dietrich discusses the importance of trust in building a PLC within the district and beyond. John Morton shares his strategy to model lifelong learning for faculty and students in the district. Other specific strategies for reaching out to the larger community are described by Robert Olsen and John Morton, while Mark Keen discusses how to work effectively with the media. In the last article, Robert E. Nicks describes programs that resulted when he emphasized building community at every level.

Building Relationships With the Board of Education

John Morton
Newton, Kansas

Good relationships are forged; they do not happen by accident. I follow several fairly simple rules that have helped me maintain a positive relationship with a variety of boards.

- *Respond to a board inquiry the same day* whenever possible. Whether it be an e-mail, telephone call, personal visit, or note, my goal is to provide a same-day response. It requires more work, but the payoff is that I don't run the risk of getting busy with other matters and forget to respond. The board must always know I am responsive to their concerns.
- *Keep the board updated.* I send an electronic Friday update to all board members with highlights of the past week's issues, always with my schedule for the following week. I make sure

they are informed in a timely manner whenever a situation arises that would call for board-level awareness.

- *Affirm the efforts of the board* frequently and publicly. Board members do a great deal and get little recognition. It is important to give the board credit for its volunteer work in furthering the cause of education in our community.
- *Model the appropriate superintendent role* for the board. I serve as a very important link between the board and the school district as well as the board and the community. It is critical that I always model the best in professionalism and practice in all these situations in my dual role.
- *Encourage board professional development.* Board members come to their elected positions with little or no formal training; they need to learn and grow professionally in their roles. I encourage the board to earn boardsmanship points by attending regional-, state-, and national-level trainings. When possible and practical, I attend with them.
- *Be a listening ear.* Sometimes all board members need is someone to listen to them in a nonjudgmental or uncritical way. When board members call, take time to listen—really listen—to their concerns.
- *Recognize the board* at district events, especially at the beginning and end of the school year. Often, district employees may neither understand nor appreciate the role of the board in the operation of the district. It is important to point out this information to the internal audience as well as to the external one.
- *Thank board members for their support* in affording you the opportunity to provide leadership for the school district.

School Board: Team of Eight Training

Chuck Holt
Lexington, Texas

School boards, like all political institutions, are full of local dynamics and are driven by the culture. Of the three tiers of board training required in Texas for board members, I find the most important to be the Team of Eight Training. The instruction in the areas of trust, cooperation, and how to function as a team is probably more important to the success of a board than any other training members routinely receive. Policy, legislation, and funding issues change often and are just part and parcel of most institutions. Whether or not a board can make positive changes in a district is much more complicated, however, because it is often driven by human elements, including cooperation.

We confidentially survey board members to evaluate how well they believe they work on a team. I like to request that the outside trainer complete this survey prior to the actual training meeting so that they understand the board members' feelings. This training is always separate from any other meeting or agenda item and is preceded by a special dinner. I believe it is important to set the tone for this meeting and to hold it away from the normal environs of the board, if possible. A retreat location like a community center or summer camp facility is optimal. Trainers should be selected who are respected by the board members and possess public school expertise. Although this training will not guarantee that board members will always function within their roles and cooperate appropriately, it will bring the need to work together directly to their attention on a yearly basis. I often refer to the training points throughout the year to remind members of the importance to the district of being a team and not seven individual members.

Everyone Is Important

Robert Olsen
Sturgis, Michigan

In a school district, the fact that the bus driver effectively and with great energy greets children each morning and literally helps create the positive climate for that child's successful day . . . is just as important to the organization as the Advanced Placement teacher preparing seniors for college placement. Great school districts understand and practice that kind of working relationship.

Creating a Professional Learning Community

Brian Knutson
Lake Zurich, Illinois

In November 2003, I began my research on Community Unit School District 95 in Lake Zurich, Illinois, as part of my preparation for applying for the superintendent opening. I discovered that Lake Zurich had a good reputation for quality education with those who really looked for quality schools but was not as well known as some of the other school districts also located in prestigious Lake County in the northwest suburbs of Chicago. Upon my arrival in April 2004, I immediately started calling us the hidden jewel of Lake County.

Beginning with my interview with the school board in November, I started planting the seeds for developing a Professional Learning Community (PLC) in Lake Zurich. From some of the research I had done, I felt that a PLC was the best vehicle for building and sustaining meaningful change in my new district.

I began developing that mindset with our district leadership team (DLT) by leading a book study. Our DLT studied *Professional Learning Communities at Work* by Richard DuFour and Robert Eaker. I really believe that this book can help a new superintendent or principal create a focus and put together a road map for sustained change. In the following paragraphs, I share the journey our high school has followed to that end and how we are using similar strategies for success in each of our other schools. Our goal in that journey is to always focus on these four key questions:

1. What is it we expect students to learn?

2. How will we know when students have learned it?

3. How will we respond when students don't learn?

4. How will we respond when students already know it?

Our new high school principal, Dr. Mike Egan, began the PLC journey in the 2004–2005 school year. He used a fairly common path by working with his staff to create a common mission—Why do we exist?—and a common vision—What do we hope to become? We used our first School Improvement Institute Day in September 2004 to engage the staff in that dialog. The staff broke into small groups to discuss answers to the following questions:

1. What is our purpose as a school?

2. What would we like our school to become?

3. What could we accomplish in the next five years that would make us proud?

4. What additions would you make to the vision and goals?

5. How do the vision and goals apply to what we are currently doing at Lake Zurich High School?

6. What are you currently doing in your classroom that supports the vision and goals?

7. Is there a strategy or instructional technique you would like to experiment with that is in line with the stated vision and goals?

8. What support would you need to implement the concepts and strategies outlined in the vision and goals?

9. When you are asked to assist in implementing the vision and goals, what do you see as your role?

10. Describe how Lake Zurich High School can function better as a PLC? What are the key characteristics?

Following this activity, a steering committee was put together comprised of volunteers from the staff. The committee members read professional literature, attended conferences, and visited schools as part of their studies. They then modified the school's mission and vision, established goals, and drafted an implementation plan.

The following goals were established as part of that process by the school leadership team and staff:

1. Increase the ACT Composite score from 22.4 (2004) to 24.1 over the next five years. (The 2008 score was 23.7, with an increase in the number of students taking the test.)

2. Establish and implement classroom/departmental performance criteria.

3. Train all teachers to utilize educational research in developing and implementing best instructional practices.

4. Utilize data analysis by teachers and department chairs to improve student achievement.

5. Research, develop, and implement a developmental guidance program with junior/senior emphasis on college/career planning to provide students direction and support in their academic pursuits at Lake Zurich High School and beyond.

The journey at Lake Zurich High School and our other schools in Lake Zurich continues as we work collaboratively to build a PLC culture. I have been fortunate in having a principal willing to take a risk in his first year as principal and in having other principals and administrators embrace this vision of a PLC culture. Our district administrative team provided the support and encouragement to begin and continue the journey. There have been many paths taken in that journey, and we are making progress in creating sustained change to enhance student learning. We also work collaboratively in building trust with our teacher association to help in this change process. Throughout this journey, we continue to focus on the four key questions mentioned earlier that focus on student expectations for learning, on knowing when learning has occurred and when it has not occurred, and on how we respond to these student needs.

Building Community: Three Key Elements and Four Steps to Implement

Thomas Little
Indianapolis, Indiana

The term *community* as used here is defined as a group of people within an organization that has embraced a common philosophical belief. The development of a sense of community within the framework of the schoolhouse does not occur overnight, nor by accident. Building a spirit of community within an educational setting is an evolutionary process; it grows and matures over time through methodical, planned stages.

THREE KEY ELEMENTS

The three key elements to the successful establishment of an effective and supportive community are trust, respect, and communication. These key elements provide a foundation for a community of support that ultimately focuses on a common mission and vision for the organization. The commitment of the members of the organization to a common mission and vision forms a common philosophical leadership base to provide direction as well as a focus to measure success.

The ability of members of the community to trust each other is vital to establishing a sense of community. The level of trust in an organization can be measured in the way the members of the organization make decisions. The level of trust within the organization is strong if individual members are able to voice their dissention to issues, freely express their opinions, and yet in the final analysis reach a decision that all members of the organization can support. Trust of the leadership is vital if a common focus is to develop within the community. One step we followed in our district to achieve this level of trust was to establish a set of core values, which I have embraced in my personal as well as professional life. I describe these core values as our commitments as employees in this district. I hold myself, as well as those who are a part of our organizational family, accountable to the following commitments:

- Commitment to your moral compass
- Commitment to your family
- Commitment to yourself—both physically and mentally
- Commitment to the children placed under your care
- Commitment to those you supervise
- Commitment to those who supervise you

The ability of members of the organization to respect each other is also important in the formation of a community. The respect exhibited among the membership of the organization enables the group to focus on a common success goal, established by the leadership in collaboration with the community. The level of respect within the organization is strong if individual members make supportive comments and acknowledge differences in opinions. The ability to disagree in an agreeable fashion is a cornerstone in the development of a community. In our district, we develop respect for one another by confronting all issues in a fashion that is open, honest, and forthright. Staff members understand that mistakes can be and will be made in an organization that fosters creativity and experimentation. Staff members also understand that mistakes are part of the growth process and, as long as those mistakes are not immoral, illegal, or unethical, there is nothing that cannot be addressed, redirected, and rectified.

Communication that flows freely among the members of the organization builds a sense of security that assists in developing common success goals to solidify the concept of community. Information that is shared by all establishes a common understanding of the challenges faced within the organization. Common knowledge and information bases develop into a common identity, which in turn develops a community base. In our district, we communicate issues to our staff before they learn this information from the media. All staff members receive weekly communications through a district newsletter on the positive aspects of the district as well as the challenges we face.

STEPS TO IMPLEMENTATION

The first step in the development of community begins to evolve during the selection process for a leader of an organization. This process must contain relevant input from the community, which will be directly affected by the candidate selection. The community must have a sense that its specific needs will be considered during the interview process. When a group from the community plays a significant role in the selection of a leader, it will provide support to that leadership afterward. One way we involved the community in this process was to hold community forums prior to the selection of a superintendent of schools to obtain perspectives on the qualities of an effective leader. The second step in the development of community follows immediately after the leader has been selected for the position. The initial contacts with the media and the tone that the superintendent portrays begin to form a sense of identity for the leadership of the organization. The initial impressions of the organization by the leader as well as the vision that the leader holds for the organization formulate the foundation of a community. In our district, all press releases and commentary from the newly appointed superintendent are framed within the goal of meeting the needs of children based on a relationship perspective. We consistently communicate with our community that our children are human beings at the forefront of our thinking. This common thread was voiced by our community as a quality it wanted in a superintendent of schools.

The third step encompasses building relationships with key members within the parameters of the community. Typically, those individuals with formally appointed power and informal power should be initially contacted. Opening the lines of communication among those individuals will begin to establish a common understanding of the needs and focus of the educational community. To accomplish this step, I schedule and plan individual and group meetings that will develop an understanding of the culture of the organization and provide the leadership with an understanding of current needs. Our school board members developed a list of fifty key communicators within the school district who had power and influence in various segments of our community. Representatives of government, local unions, local business operations, as well as the teacher association are examples of targeted groups. These individuals were personally contacted, and meetings were structured to focus upon two key questions. The first question was meant to uncover what was believed to be the key components currently existing within the organization that should never be changed, and why. The second question focused on what key components in the organization should be changed as soon as possible, and individuals were asked to provide a rationale for the needed change. This approach not only provided a great deal of information about the district but also began to build a support base for future initiatives by this community.

The fourth step entails a formalized development of the mission and vision statements for the organization, which provide direction and a common bond among the members of the community. The leadership is now in a position to develop goals and objectives that will reflect a sense of the community. The collective work in meeting those common goals and objectives will continue building that sense of community as it supports the success of the organization. The mission and vision statements within the organization will drive every decision made in the district. The goals and objectives that evolve from this process will be formulated into a strategic plan for the next five years that can be adopted and embraced by the whole school community. This strategic plan is revisited on an annual basis and revised for the upcoming years as needs change and evolve.

Communicating and Collaborating Within the District Takes Effort

Paul Kinder
Blue Springs, Missouri

In today's educational culture, the need for communication and collaboration is extremely important if not essential to the success of the organization. This communication and collaboration can only be achieved by extensive work, time, and energy; however, the results will more than outweigh the effort. In the Blue Springs (MO) School District, collaboration starts with leadership team meetings every Monday morning that include the superintendent, deputy super-intendent, assistant superintendent of human resources, assistant superintendent of administration, assistant superintendent of manage-ment services, chief financial officer, assistant to the superintendent for student and community relations, and the director of public relations/information. Administrators on the leadership team use this time to discuss the projects under their supervision and seek feedback from their colleagues. Goal-setting and program evaluations are a valuable part of this collaborative time. This meeting is a productive beginning to each week for the leadership team and district as a whole.

The Blue Springs School District has twenty-two school sites. Communication with each of those sites is essential to the success of our district. As superintendent of schools, I meet twice a year with an advisory group in each building. I also have lunch twice each year in each building, where I spend the entire lunch period in the staff workroom visiting with all members of that school. Additionally, a teacher advisory group comprised of one representative from each building meets three times per year with me and members of our leadership team.

To enhance one-on-one communication, I also hand deliver the first paycheck of the year to each certified and noncertified staff member in September and again in December prior to the holiday break. This task is rather daunting because we employ approxi-mately 2,000 people; however, it has been beneficial. It is a great way for me to have the opportunity to see the staff members, even if only for a few seconds. These face-to-face talks help not only with communication but also with the comfort level between the building staff and leadership of our district.

We also use various forms of written communication to our staff on a regular basis. Our Friday publication is called the *IN* or *Information Network*. It is distributed to all staff members and talks about staff issues from the past week, including but not limited to the following: death of family members, medical issues, congratulations to any employee given awards or a family member given awards dur-ing the past week, birth of employee staff members' babies as well as grandchildren, information about activities for the upcoming week such as school plays and athletic events, a job listing of available positions, and something we call the "Trading Post"—a way for staff members to advertise items they have for sale.

We also have an *On Board* publication e-mailed to all staff members the day after every board of education meeting that highlights what happened at the board meeting the night before. During the state legislative session, from January through the middle of May, we do a "Friday Legislative Update" that is sent through our e-mail to all staff members and highlights what happened in our state capitol the previous week.

Finally, four times per year, as the name implies, we publish the *Information Quarterly* or *IQ,* which highlights happenings in the district such as visitors or guests we have had during the previous few weeks, upcoming district events that may be occurring, and student successes.

The Blue Springs R-IV School District continues to work very hard every day on communication and collaboration with our staff to ensure trust and a feeling of belonging, which we know is essential to the overall structure and success of the district.

Building Trust in the Community at Every Level

Brenda Dietrich
Topeka, Kansas

The Auburn-Washburn School District has a collaborative working environment focused on improving teaching and learning. I have been in the district for seven years now. When I first arrived, the district had totally embraced and was very proud of its site-based operational model. The buildings and principals were very autonomous and more competitive than I was comfortable with when trying to build a team that functioned with a high degree of trust. My approach to district operations was a bit different. I certainly supported some of the tenets of site-based management, but I strongly believed that, if we were going to do our best work, we must have a collaborative environment characterized by open dialog and trusting relationships. My experiences as a school district administrator over fifteen years had solidified my belief that collaboration is a very powerful tool for accomplishing our mutually defined and agreed-upon goals.

To be successful, I felt we needed to be much closer as a work group, and it was my job to create a high-performing team. I worked hard to build relationships with staff, students, parents, patrons, city, county, and even state officials, especially since we are located in Topeka, the heart of state government in Kansas. We are blessed with a board of education that is very professional and makes thoughtful and rational decisions. The board is always very student centered. I needed the administrative team to function as a team and be able to support each other and the board as we refined our district mission, vision, core values, and, ultimately, our strategic plan.

We worked together very hard to set SMART (specific, measurable, attainable, realistic, timely) goals (Nelson, Economy, & Blanchard, 2003). We made sure that our strategic plan was written in the SMART goal format. Using this process made it very easy to understand the tasks and goals that had to be accomplished throughout the year. We divided the strategic plan into areas of responsibility so it was clear who was responsible for accomplishing each goal. We communicated our progress in an annual report to the public, which is now published in the district publication, *School News,* mailed to each home in the district.

The annual report allows us to be transparent and accountable to our patrons. We include our current demographic information, budget expenditures, assessment results, revenue streams, and any accomplishments or awards students and staff have received during the year. Check marks are next to the goals on the strategic plan that have been accomplished. If a goal hasn't been accomplished, we include an explanation as to its status. For example, it might be an ongoing project, and something more needs to be done before we can say the goal has been successfully accomplished. Everyone in the community knows what we are doing, how we are doing it, and who is responsible for doing it. In this way, they are able to follow our progress, and we are held accountable to our taxpayers in a formal document. It's very clear the district is serious about improving student learning and using taxpayer dollars wisely.

Another thing we do very well and often is talk and listen to the community. We began working on our strategic plan four years ago and used a focus group model. We went out into the greater Topeka area, asked for feedback, and listened to the responses. These focus groups told us what they wanted us to be working on, the kinds of things we were doing well, what we needed to improve, and skills they thought students needed to be successful in the twenty-first century. We listened to at least 400 individuals in the community—not only parents but others outside the district boundaries such as corporate leaders and higher education instructors. We used a script and asked the same specific questions of all groups. We listened to their responses, identified trends, revised our mission, vision, and core values, and developed a five-year strategic plan. The strategic plan defines our goals and contains a timeline that guides our work each year.

The board identified larger initiatives that also became a large part of our strategic plan. Our highest-priority initiatives are focused on improving student learning or improving school climate and operations. Our work and our strategic plan is very student focused. This experience was great for all of us. Because we listened so well four years ago and created a strategic plan based on patron input, I think the bond election was successful. When you build trust with people in the community, they know you are spending their tax dollars wisely and doing all you can to ensure that the children they send to you each and every day will be successful.

Leading by Example

John Morton
Newton, Kansas

Leadership has changed dramatically both in scope and focus during my forty years as a career educational leader. A superintendent's reaction to change can lead to exhilaration or despair. Gone are the days of the academic dictator or even the benevolent autocrat. Leadership is highly dynamic, shared, and empowering. The ability to lead by example is critical; the ability to empower others even more essential.

Part of the joy of my leadership role comes from my work as an adjunct professor in the building-level and district-level leadership programs at Friends University in Wichita, Kansas. Working with aspiring leaders inspires me to be a better leader while finding ways to nurture potential leaders. I truly have the best job in my community! I facilitate learning at all levels within the school district—preparing our students for future success, supporting our staff as they craft the art of teaching and learning, and guiding our administrators as they work with the very challenging circumstances in today's complex world of education.

We expect our students to become lifelong learners, and we provide opportunities for continuous learning for staff and administrators. Sometimes, however, we neglect the obvious—our own learning. To be effective leaders, we also must be effective learners. As superintendent, I have been blessed with rich and rewarding opportunities, both professional and personal.

In recent years, two experiences stand out: my participation as a member of the Kauffman Foundation Kansas/Missouri Superintendents' Forum and my involvement with our teachers and administrators in four critical strands of professional development identified as part of our district vision for excellence: Cognitive Coaching, Mentoring Matters, Data-Driven Decision-Making, and Adaptive Schools. It is critical for superintendents to lead by example. Never ask staff to undertake training you are not willing to experience as well. All training not only heightens your credibility but provides a much greater understanding of the experience and its influence upon the total school district.

Reaching Out to the Larger Community

Robert Olsen
Sturgis, Michigan

In Sturgis, as in most communities our size, the schools perform a huge role in the fabric of life throughout the area. As such, we take our commitment to community very seriously. Literally every decision our board makes is considered within the context of what is in the best interest of children, parents, staff, and community.

Sturgis is fortunate to have a number of outstanding community assets: an outstanding school district, our own electric power plant, a state-of-the-art hospital, a fully operational civic auditorium, a city-owned and -operated fitness club, wonderful parks, and residents who take great pride in the legacy that has made Sturgis what it is.

Sturgis Public Schools represent a significant community asset as a social focal point for parents and family, an economic force, and, at times, a lightning rod on issues deemed controversial to many in the community. We have consequently developed a close working relationship with our city's administration and its elected commissioners along with direct involvement with our local chamber of commerce.

Our board of education understands, appreciates, and supports the civic role the schools play in Sturgis. Although we don't always see eye to eye on all issues, through regularly scheduled joint meetings with the city commission our board has been able to play an increasingly important role in the leadership of the greater community.

We focus most of our energy, however, on school-related issues. Our primary mission is to provide an outstanding school experience for children—kindergarten through grade twelve. Additionally, we offer programs for preschool children—birth through age five—and for adults in need of high school completion and beyond.

Because of our board's commitment to the larger community, however, we have created and will continue to support three rather unique programs that are living examples of the nature of our civic mission. The Family Connection Office, the Office of Youth and Family Services, and the Sturgis Area Business Education Alliance (SABEA) are powerful examples of how this school district has fulfilled its civic responsibility above and beyond its primary mission. Through effective management of resources and outstanding organizational stewardship, our school district has become a force in meeting the needs of the entire community.

The Family Connection Office is staffed by a coordinator who manages an organized outreach program to encourage community participation in the schools. At the same time, the office organizes and manages community initiatives that, although not directly related to the school, have the potential to enhance the pool of leadership talent in the community. In conjunction with a number of other local agencies, the Family Connection Office plans and manages a wide variety of events attractive to students, parents, and residents at large.

The primary mission of the Office of Youth and Family Service is to provide leadership for the creation and implementation of programs designed to enhance and increase the assets of our community. The office is most effective in providing startup leadership and a helping hand to sustain projects that add quality to the fabric of life in our community. Sturgis Public Schools thus accomplishes the following:

- Provides community safety programs
- Promotes networking for businesses and industries
- Implements health and safety information for the community
- Provides and promotes opportunities for community involvement for youth
- Provides alternative activities for youth
- Promotes and provides parenting classes

And last, our SABEA initiative has established an incredibly strong working relationship with our business community. Working under the direction of SABEA, the career pathways coordinators have worked relentlessly to engage the business and industrial community. Approximately 200 business partners visit and team teach with each of our teaching staff on a monthly basis. An equal number engages in the evaluation of portfolio presentations given by seniors as part of our graduation requirements.

I have worked in school districts in six different communities in Michigan and have never experienced the breadth and depth of school community interaction and cooperation that I have experienced here. Doing things for the greater good is not just a slogan in the Sturgis Public Schools; it is a way of life.

The Expanding Role of Community

John Morton
Newton, Kansas

Perhaps no role has expanded more dramatically for superintendents than that of reaching into the community. Educating, motivating, explaining, and supporting education at the grassroots level is an imperative, not only at the local community level but at the state and national levels as well. My job has taken on more political overtones than I ever imagined in my early years as an administrator. Interfacing with governmental bodies, legislators, state board members, and members of a myriad of professional and service organizations has become a priority. I am often called upon to provide key information relative to critical issues in the Newton community. I make myself readily available to speak to community groups and service organizations.

The community also consists of private schools and homeschooled students. I make it a point to touch base with all of our private schools in the area to see how we might be helpful to them and their students. One of these visits resulted in our district providing art, music, and physical education experiences for our local K–8 Catholic school. I have also made it a very simple process for out-of-district students to attend our district and for homeschooled students to take parts of their academic work through our district. Schools are an inherent part of the larger community, and we must be active, not passive, participants in the endeavor to create community partnerships to maximize educational opportunities and support for all students.

Maintaining Quality Media Relationships

Mark Keen
Westfield, Indiana

The media can be a source of support and an opportunity for you to enhance a message, or it can be a constant source of irritation. How you view and approach your relationship with the media is dependent upon your attitude. Although not comprehensive, here are some major factors to keep in mind when formulating your approach to media relations:

- It's their job. Reporters need and want information and stories. You can be a source for these or an obstacle.
- The media can get your message out to more people than you can.
- Taking time to explain things thoroughly to achieve understanding leads to better information.
- "Unavailable for comment" or "no comment" usually carries a negative connotation.

I will readily admit that my stomach tightens a little when a reporter calls to talk with me. I make what is probably a fairly normal assumption that "something's wrong." In 99 percent of the cases, however, this is not what the call is about. The reporter is usually calling to obtain information or comparative data for a story he or she is working on.

So, what are some ways to help reporters get their stories? One way is to enlist the aid of the building principals to alert you to events that might be newsworthy. Reporters love pictures of children, whether on camera or in print. Don't assume the media will not be interested; let them make the call. Events are covered on slow news days that might be ignored at other times.

Another way is to be inviting. I always stay around in the room after a board meeting to answer any questions the media have, and I make sure to invite a reporter to call me if any questions come up while the story is being written. I'm fortunate enough to have an excellent community relations director, and she sometimes provides information prior to the meeting on certain topics to try to direct the story line.

I have the philosophy that anything reporters ask for or ask about (unless legally protected) is given to them or responded to as quickly as possible. I never want to convey that anything is hidden, unknown, or being avoided. Occasionally, a reporter has called with a last-minute request for a comment or information that has resulted in some pressure, but overall the relationship I have built with journalists has been well worth the effort.

When asked for an interview, I try to ask for the questions ahead of time. This permits me to get specific information, if necessary, and also makes the interview flow. If the interview is on camera, it helps me avoid the "deer in the headlights" look.

It is amazing how little people in the media understand about the K–12 world. Unwittingly, I initially assumed a lot when answering questions and couldn't understand why they didn't "get it." They did "get it," from their knowledge base, so it is very important to explain more rather than less. Although there is never any guarantee that the story will be 100 percent correct, taking the time to explain increases the chance that it will. Also, remember that the reporters write the story; the editors write the headline for it; often there is no connection between the two. Reporters are appreciative when you understand that fact.

Occasionally, when a news crew is in the area, a reporter will call to find out if anything is going on in a school he or she may want to cover. These calls normally come from people we've worked with over the years, and we have gotten some good coverage on a number of occasions.

I asked two local reporters to give me thoughts they would like to convey to new superintendents about working with the media. Here is what they came up with (some of which may be surprising):

- Invite reporters in when *good* things are happening. If a staff member is going to be recognized with a major award, even though the name of the person receiving the award may still be confidential, you can nevertheless call and invite the reporter saying an event is scheduled and he or she may want to attend. Better yet, if you've developed trust with the reporter, provide the information under an embargo. This allows the reporter time to prepare, gets the district in the news for happenings, and builds a good working relationship.
- Return reporters' calls, or have someone call for you. This simple courtesy ensures good relationships.
- If, when you return a call, you find that you don't have sufficient time to respond right then, ascertain the reporter's deadline and how much time the reporter might need with you.
- Don't lie, ever! If a reporter asks a question and you don't know the answer, admit it and offer to get the information or get the reporter in touch with the person who has the information. Finding out that a response was a half-truth or a lie destroys all future credibility.
- The reporter is not the enemy. Try to load the reporter up with as much good news as possible and don't try to hide the less favorable stuff. At the end of the day, the good coverage almost always outweighs the bad or uncomfortable coverage, especially when good and open lines of communication have been established.

An extremely good reference book is *How to Sell Yourself* by Arch Lustberg (2008). In fact, if you have the opportunity to attend one of his workshops, it's an investment that will definitely pay off. One of his ideas is to try to control the message and not to push the message the media is interested in. For example, if the reporter (print or TV) asks, "Why are your schools failing?" and you respond, "Our schools are not failing, but . . . ," the listener has heard "schools" and "failing" twice, and you have reinforced the negative thought. Instead, the response could be, "Let me tell you of our schools' successes . . . ," thus changing a negative to a positive response. Politicians do this all the time. Often you feel the need to respond quickly to a question when the better approach is to focus your message rather than simply responding.

Another great idea that I took away from Arch's workshop was to create our own set of "buzz words." These key words and phrases describe our area of emphasis so that all administrators, and eventually many teachers, begin to repeat these "buzz words" to communicate our preferred message. Again, this way we control the message rather than have others control it for us. Right now, we are aligning our district systems using the Baldrige criteria. Rather than refer to Baldrige, however, which might cause skeptics to say we're only interested in the award, we choose to use as our buzz words "continuous quality growth." Not only does this phrase get away from using the term Baldridge but it conveys a powerful message to staff, parents, and other community members.

Your attitude toward the media will affect how well you work with them. If you distrust and interact with them as little as possible, you will gain little from the relationship. If you view the media as partners who can help your district, much can be gained in the long run.

Building Community by Developing Cost-Effective Partnerships

Robert E. Nicks
Beaumont, Texas

West Texas is a vast area, rich with oil and natural gas reserves, lots of sunshine, and industrious people who have an independent spirit—a spirit undoubtedly influenced by early settlers who shared their resources and labor to work the land and cattle. The cooperation exhibited by pioneer residents was as necessary as water in the high desert for survival and is still evident in the Midland Independent School District and the community it serves.

Midland, Texas, is located on Interstate 20, halfway between Dallas and El Paso. The city has a population of 100,000, and the school district includes the city and a surrounding 700 square miles of sparsely populated area. The school district has approximately 21,000 students and enjoys great support by the community, philanthropic foundations, and public entities.

One of my most effective practices as a superintendent has been in developing partnerships for shared programs and facilities that have enriched the school district beyond what could have been provided with school district resources. As you read the following examples of partnerships between Midland ISD, city government,

Midland College, and local organizations, think of your own school district and the resources that might be available in your community. What partnerships might be forged to provide programs or facilities to enhance the quality of education for your students?

Will Someone Share the Cost of the New Football Stadium, Please?

The school district's existing high school football stadium did not have adequate parking or seating capacity, was not ADA compliant, and was generally inadequate by all measurement standards. A new football/soccer stadium was needed, and a public referendum (facility bond issue) would be a necessity due to the projected cost of approximately $20 million. The city of Midland also wanted to build a new stadium for the "AA" professional baseball team that played in the city. The result was an agreement between city government and the school district wherein the city would build both stadiums. The city would own the facilities, and a long-term lease with the school district would provide a source of income to maintain the football/soccer stadium. When Midland ISD is not using the stadium, the city has the option to rent the facility for other activities— playoff games, exhibitions, concerts, and so on. This collaborative approach resulted in voter approval for a facility that serves the entire community.

Can We Play in Your College Gymnasium?

When Midland College sought community support to build a new activities center, it was suggested that taxpayers would prefer to have one outstanding facility for college and high school sports events instead of multiple facilities throughout the city. Today, Midland College, Robert E. Lee HS, and Midland HS play their boys' and girls' varsity basketball games in the Chaparral Center on the Midland College campus. The facility was built with a Midland College bond issue and is a beautiful building with a capacity of approximately 5,000 spectators. School district convocation, concerts, graduation ceremonies, and other special events are also held in the facility. Are there times when schedule conflicts occur? Of course, but the school district and the college have developed an excellent working relationship, and with the exception of the occasional tournament, sports teams at the high schools and college play on different days of the week. Constituents see this partnership as extremely cost-effective.

ORCHESTRA CLASSES IN ELEMENTARY SCHOOLS—HOW CAN YOU FIND QUALIFIED TEACHERS?

Midland ISD has worked with the Midland-Odessa Symphony for many years in a collaborative effort that has benefited both organizations. To attract professional musicians to play in the regional symphony orchestra, musicians are given an opportunity to supplement their orchestra salary. An agreement was developed to assist the orchestra and the school district. A "Strings Program" was initiated at elementary campuses in the school district, and professional musicians are hired to teach the classes. The program is affordable since teachers are assigned to multiple campuses and teach small groups of interested students.

Teaching stringed instruments to students at an early age enriches the school district's performing arts instruction, and the program is used as a recruitment strategy by the regional symphony. It is a partnership that serves the purposes of both organizations and is providing performing arts opportunities that help meet the expectations of the community.

COULD THAT ABANDONED BUILDING REALLY BECOME A TECHNOLOGY CENTER?

The Work Force Commission needed a technology center to train workers new to the area and to improve the skills of those in the existing workforce. Midland College needed additional training facilities and computer labs. Midland ISD needed computer labs and greater access to college courses so that students could take "dual credit" courses that earn both high school and college credit. The result was an agreement to purchase an abandoned retail building and generate a capital fundraising effort in the community to match the contributions of participating public entities. The cooperative effort renovated a part of the city that needed economic development and provided a great facility for training and learning.

The Advanced Technology Center (ATC) provides classrooms, computer labs, and training facilities during the day, primarily for use by high school students, and evening classes for college students and workforce training. The facility is utilized most weekends as well since many companies will schedule the building for company events and training. Much of the $6 million dedicated to renovating the facility came from philanthropic organizations and individuals within the community who saw the value of collaboration and cost sharing. A contribution of $1 million by Midland ISD and Midland College has resulted in a facility worth many times that investment and has added new educational opportunities for students.

SHARE THE COST OF TENNIS, ANYONE?

The city of Midland, like most cities, sponsors a summer recreational program for young people and adults. Tennis is an important activity in that summer program, and tennis courts are needed. It is only natural to ask the question, "Is there a way to share high school tennis facilities during the summer and meet the needs of the summer program and high school needs?" In Midland, that answer is "yes."

The cost-sharing partnership between the school district and the city allows the city to pay for major renovations and the school district to pay for regular maintenance items. The school schedules court use during the school year, and the city performs the same function during the summer. It is amazing how well cooperative management can work once guidelines are established and everyone becomes accustomed to the partnership. Sharing costs and responsibilities makes sense.

DOES SEPARATION OF CHURCH AND STATE MEAN VOLLEYBALL, TOO?

Across the street from Midland HS is the First Presbyterian Church. Midland is fortunate to have many fine churches that are supportive of the school district and partners to many of the campuses. If you have ever been a high school administrator, you know that there are never enough gymnasiums to accommodate the many teams that need practice and game facilities. The First Presbyterian Church partners with Midland HS by allowing the school to use its gymnasium and has provided classrooms when the campus was being renovated. The congregation has opened its doors to benefit students in more ways than one. Once each week the church offers a pizza lunch to students, and over the years a bond has developed that is very special. The separation of church and state is about religious freedom, but there is appropriate flexibility for schools and churches to partner when both are interested in what is best for students. What are the possibilities in your community?

SUMMARY

Research on Community Building

Shared leadership, trust, open communication, team building, effective decision making that involves all stakeholders, and continued lifelong learning.

Best Practice Ideas for Community Building

- Build relationships with staff, students, parents, patrons, and state officials
- Set SMART goals
- Conduct workshops to engage the community in shaping shared district outcomes
- Collaborate and communicate with community organizations frequently
- Nurture relationships with private school and homeschool constituents
- Conduct service projects
- Develop positive relationships with the media
- Hold leadership team meetings
- Build relationships with the school board
- Provide school board training
- Collaborate on the budget with the school board
- Model teamwork
- Develop cost-effective partnerships with area business

COMMUNITY BUILDING REFLECTION

1. Describe how you build community with each of the following stakeholders: school board? faculty? students? parents? the larger community?

2. How do you build community when you emphasize shared goals?

3. In what areas are you weak as a builder of community?

4. In what areas are you strong as a builder of community?

5. What are your communication strengths?

6. In what ways are you weak in communication skills?

7. Write a prescription for improvement for you to be more adept at building community.

8. What ideas in this chapter were the most important for your school?

9. How can you implement or revise ideas in this chapter to improve the feeling of community?

ADDITIONAL RESOURCES

Baldrige. http://www.baldrige.com/
Character Counts. http://charactercounts.org/
Jump Rope for Heart. http://www.aahperd.org/jump
Kids Voting Kansas. http://www.kidsvotingkansas.org
Model UN. http://www.unausa.org/site/pp.asp?c+fvKR18MPJpF&b=482843
Pennies for Patients. http://www.schoolandyouth.org/Controller?action=load
    Content&itemid+91060
SMART goals. http://wwwtopachievement.com/smart.html
Team of Eight Training. http://www.tea.state.tx.us/press/pr000204.html
Toys for Tots. http://www.toysfortots.org
Young Republican's Club. http://www.nyyrc.com

CHAPTER FOUR

Changing Times

The times they are a-changin'.

—Bob Dylan, 1964

Change is an inevitable journey. All things are constantly changing, transforming, becoming something differ-ent. . . . Indeed, the measure of a leader may well be her or his capacity to understand and deal successfully with change.

—California School Leadership Academy

Our changing times are reflected everywhere, from the demo-graphics of the workplace to those of our schools. For example, of the Americans aged sixty-five and older, 82 percent are non-Hispanic whites, only 6 percent is Hispanic, and 12 percent represent other races. However, only 58.9 percent of Americans under eighteen are white, whereas 19.2 percent are Hispanic and 22 percent com-prise other minorities. In fact, the population of Hispanics and Asians is growing at more than ten times the pace of the white sector (El Nasser & Grant, 2005), while African American and Native American school-aged populations are predicted to remain relatively stable (Carter, 2003). Despite this diversity of population, research has shown that black and Latino students have become more segregated than at any time in the last thirty years (Fears, 2001).

Changes in family structure are also occurring. Today, less than one-fourth of U.S. households are made up of married couples with children under age eighteen; single mothers head 7.2 percent of households, and few children have a caregiver who does not work outside the home (Trotter, 2001). Poverty is another concern. Nearly one in five children in the United States lives in poverty, and extreme poverty is becoming more concentrated in some inner cities (Olson, 2000). For all groups of students except white students, racially segregated schools (which are increasing in the United States) generally have high concentrations of poverty (Orfield, 2001).

The achievement gap between minority and white students continues. Darling-Hammond (2007) reported that, on national assessments in reading, writing, mathematics, and science, black students' performance lags behind that of white students and in some cases has actually declined since 1988. In 2002, the average black or Hispanic twelfth grader read at the level of the average white eighth grader (National Center for Education Statistics, 2005).

There are many cultural challenges that districts are unprepared to handle that must be faced in this time of change. For example, only 2.5 percent of English language teachers receive the specialized training needed to help today's limited or non-English-speaking students (Ruiz-de-Velasco, Fix, & Clewell, 2000). Orfield and Yun (1999) reported that African American and Hispanic students with limited English-speaking abilities are more likely to live in urban areas where schools tend to be overcrowded and have limited resources compared to majority white suburban school districts. Non-English-speaking students are likely to live in areas where there is little interaction with native English speakers and no access to private tutors or computers connected to the Internet (Suarez-Orozco & Todorova, 2003). Many studies indicate poor achievement levels among African American males (Tatum, 2006).

Another challenge to overcome is the low representation of minority administrators, with less than 5 percent of superintendent positions held by men and women of color across the United States (American Association of School Administrators, 2000). Superintendents must thus look very carefully into their own assumptions about the students in their district and be willing to pursue effective ways to successfully educate all students from every ethnic and social background; they must become culturally proficient leaders (Lindsey, Roberts, & Campbell-Jones, 2005). Superintendents who urgently commit to this task are more likely to lead districts where all populations of students achieve academically (Price & Harris, 2008).

In the submissions that follow, award-winning superintendents address specific programs they implemented to support students during this time of change. Robert Olsen discusses the changing nature of the superintendency in the twenty-first century. Pauline Hargrove challenges superintendents to build relationships to navigate successfully through this time of change. A renewed curricular commitment to engage students in civic education is suggested by Brenda Dietrich as being a support to students during these changing times, and Michael McGill describes what his district is doing to prepare young people in today's global community by infusing the curriculum with a global emphasis. The last article in this chapter is by Jerry L. Patterson and Diane E. Reed. They describe ten strengths of superintendents that lead to resiliency and the courage to tackle the seemingly overwhelming problems of educating students today.

The Changing Nature of Today's Superintendency

Robert Olsen
Sturgis, Michigan

The way in which school success is measured has gone through dramatic and, for the most part, necessary change. Our public, the education community, and the political establishment on both sides of the aisle are measuring success in ways dramatically different from the past. Where school district success was once measured in terms of inputs, it is now measured in terms of outcomes—for the most part, academic outcomes. It is simply no longer enough to brag about a solid budget, wonderful facilities, and the best of resources. Although wins on the athletic field and honors for bands and choirs are still a huge source of community and school pride, academic achievement has now trumped all else when it comes to bragging rights over the comparative quality of schools. If you are not producing great test scores and churning out National Merit semifinalists, you are no longer considered to be making the grade.

I would have to say that, in my relatively short tenure as superintendent, I have witnessed and experienced a significant shift in expectations for the position. The same skill set and target goals that once were acceptable and appropriate are simply not enough anymore. Similar to other professional leadership positions, the superintendency has become more about short-term academic productivity and related efficiencies rather than about strong, academic programming that produced sound thinkers and solid citizens. And if you are not producing, you will be penalized and punished quickly and severely. In many cases, there is a real "what have you done for me lately" mentality.

But I think what I have just described might be the pendulum completing its arc to one extreme and starting its descent back to the center. And my hope is that each time we experience these swings we learn a little bit more about what is in the best interest of students, teachers, schools, communities, and our nation.

As I reflect on my twenty-six years of leadership experience in education, I can't help but think about the superintendents who have mentored me and contributed so much in my development as a school leader. Although advice and support was always in abundance, I learned a great deal more by watching them work on projects of which I was an integral part, and on projects in which I had little or no connection. Working alongside six outstanding school leaders, I was able to view a huge range of management philosophies and styles. From those and other experiences, I learned things I should, and shouldn't, do!

Although the pressure for reform and continual improvement has been in many ways a good thing, it is taking its toll on the superintendency. In ways unforeseen just a few years ago, the pace, demands, and pressure to perform send mixed signals to those wanting to lead school districts. At one time, the skill set had a great deal to do with budget, personnel, and management skills rather than instructional leadership. I don't mean to imply that the superintendency was stocked with management professionals; it clearly was not. Each of the great mentors I mentioned had strong manager skills and styles but with great insight into issues related to curriculum and instruction. But the nature of the job demanded more attention to management side issues. Now, the issues are much more multifaceted, and the skill sets in greatest demand are those associated with instructional leadership.

Regardless of relative professional strengths, one must be prepared for a somewhat short, bumpy, and challenging tenure. You need to be able to perform as educational leader, budget wizard, fundraiser, economic development coordinator, marketer, motivational speaker, child advocate, parent advocate, teacher advocate, board advocate, chief negotiator, arbitrator, judge, architect, engineer, and construction manager. And if you can do all that, you get the real reward of being able to read to first graders on a moment's notice. What more could one ask?

Servant Leaders Build Relationships in Changing Times

Pauline Hargrove
Orange, Texas

As superintendent of the Little Cypress-Mauriceville CISD in Texas, I believe I should be the lead servant, lead learner, and gatekeeper for the district. I am not here to be served but to serve. The work that I do is not about me but about those I serve, beginning with God. Knowing this gives me the confidence, strength, and freedom to do what I have been called to do. In this capacity and in the changing times during which we live, the goal of my servanthood is to build strong relationships throughout the school district and larger community that will foster excellence, build goodwill, and benefit the individual and all of society.

THE SUPERINTENDENT AS LEAD SERVANT

It is my mission to do my very best to serve all students and the faculty and staff by enabling, equipping, empowering, and inspiring them to maximize their full potential to meet the challenges and attain the goals set before us. This service extends to the families of our students as well as to the community at-large and is at the pleasure of our school board of trustees. As a servant, the superintendent must know the people he or she serves to meet their needs and make a way for their success; therefore, time and effort must be dedicated to establishing caring relationships built on mutual trust and respect with a common vision. Visiting campuses on a weekly basis; attending meetings, events, and conferences; visiting with students and staff; being available on an as-needed basis; and participating in classroom, schoolwide, and districtwide activities provide superintendents with opportunities to establish relationships and stay in touch with those they serve. By being a frequent speaker, presenter, participant, and listener at school and civic events, superintendents can connect with students, parents, staff, and community members to build stronger relationships and expand their circle of influence.

THE SUPERINTENDENT AS LEAD LEARNER

It is the superintendent's responsibility and privilege to promote the goal of being a lifelong learner by being a lead learner. Leading by example provides the visual picture people need in order to follow. It is essential for one to remain current with trends, research, and best practices to lead the educational process. I thus read professional literature, listen to educational audio journals, and network with other education and business leaders. Additionally, I am an active member of professional organizations and avail myself of learning opportunities through various conferences, seminars, training sessions, and postgraduate coursework.

Continuous learning keeps our administrative team abreast of the best practices, which we implement for the benefit of our students. The administrative team participates in an annual team-building retreat in which hot topics and issues of concern are addressed, possible solutions are sought, and knowledge and skills are expanded through special presentations. For the past four years, this event has been coordinated with two other districts to allow a professional network to be established and more ideas to be generated and shared.

THE SUPERINTENDENT AS GATEKEEPER

As the gatekeeper of the district, the superintendent is responsible for what is allowed and what is prevented from entering the district. Being knowledgeable about programs, practices, procedures, individuals, and groups is a necessity. Protecting the learning environment and establishing the culture for professional learning communities are two keys for quality learning to occur at more rigorous levels. Ultimately, the positive, caring attitudes of the educators who establish relationships with one another and the students are what create the safe place where students and staff want to come to learn and work. Being present and visible, asking questions, listening, learning, and being actively engaged enable the superintendent to monitor and adjust the gate appropriately for maximum security and success.

Changing Times Emphasize a Need for Civic Education

Brenda Dietrich
Topeka, Kansas

The mission of the Auburn-Washburn School District is to deliver an exemplary, world-class education for all students, instilling in them the knowledge, skills, and character required to be responsible and productive citizens. Our schools and students are fully engaged in a variety of activities and programs that speak to the ideals of civic education and civic mission.

I have read some research recently that categorizes civic education into preparing "personally responsible" citizens and "participatory" citizens. Those categories provide a nice framework to describe how Auburn-Washburn seeks to fulfill its mission and prepare students to be competent, responsible, and productive citizens.

Personally responsible citizens are helping citizens who demonstrate social responsibility, kindness, and compassion. Our students spend thousands of hours helping others and donating their time. At the high school, we have blood drives each semester and turn our English IMC into a Red Cross blood bank. The student council at the high school organizes the drive, and in typical teenager fashion, they time it for Halloween and use unique slogans and costumes to inspire participation. Last year our high school donated more pints of blood to the Red Cross than did any other high school in our area. Our industrial arts teacher takes his woodshop students and any other student who volunteers at Washburn Rural High School with him on the weekends to build a Habitat for Humanity house in downtown Topeka. We have built a house using volunteer student (and sometimes parent) labor every year for the past eight years.

Washburn Rural Middle School has a rather unique "Kindness Unites Us" reception every other year that draws hundreds of adults and students into the gym for a special recognition. It is an extension of the Character Counts character education program in the district. The middle school students (835) are asked to write an essay about an adult in their lives who has been kind or helped them in some way. The person they write about has to be eighteen years old or older. No immediate family members or rock stars are eligible. Most often, students write about church youth leaders, coaches, family friends, teachers, or other special adults in their lives. The students then send an invitation to their "adult" asking them to come to the Kindness Unites Us program and reception. Last year guests came from ten states and from points all across Kansas to the reception. They were given a copy of the essay and treated to a musical program. The kids felt great, but their adult guests felt even better and told us it was the neatest program in which they had ever been involved.

Our students in all buildings do the traditional volunteering at soup kitchens and nursing homes. Throughout the district, we all (students and adults) participate in canned food drives and collect "pennies for patients" and Toys for Tots. Our middle schoolers collected and donated hundreds of books to school libraries in Florida and Louisiana after the recent hurricanes, and all buildings collected clothing and money for tsunami relief. Our elementary students Jump Rope for the Heart, and one of our buildings teamed with Payless Shoes, headquartered in Topeka, to distribute free shoes to needy families. Our students raise funds for Veteran's Affairs (VA in Topeka) to help them buy necessary items, and all of our bands participate in community parades. The middle school students received Integrity Counts certificates at the end of the school year based on the number of hours they volunteered in the community. At Auburn Elementary, students receive Biz Card Boost coupons that encourage good manners and citizenship and allow them to shop in the school store. Our goal is to promote the virtues of empathy, trust, benevolence, and fairness and to reward living respectfully.

Participatory citizens are actively involved in community organizations and civic affairs. We have an extensive extracurricular program at the middle school and high school where students are regularly involved in opportunities to learn and practice leadership skills and self-governance. All buildings have active student councils that allow them to engage in "democratic discourse" and decision making. At the high school, our student council registers eighteen-year-olds to vote, then rewards those students with a free cookie from the Cookie Shack (open at lunchtime) and with another cookie if they actually vote! We participate in mock elections, Model UN, and Kids Voting Kansas, and Senator Brownback's son started a

Young Republican's Club at the high school last year. Some of the more unique opportunities that we provide for students are related to economic citizenship and responsibility. Two years ago, we partnered with the Educational Credit Union and the Office of the State Treasurer to implement a banking program called "Save @ School," which has spread to all elementary buildings. Students learn valuable lessons in financial literacy that are aligned with the state math standards. The program also teaches our students practical money management skills. At the high school, we partnered with Silver Lake Bank and actually built a small extension of the bank in the commons area of the high school. The WRHS Bank is a student-run bank that is part of the business department's curriculum. We have 300 active accounts at the bank, and business is booming!

Last, I would say that the pride we instill in our students through our celebrations of Kansas history and the patriotism our students learn through their interactions with our local servicemen and women allow us to create a love for our country and a desire to be actively engaged. Our schools still say the Pledge of Allegiance every morning, and our band proudly plays the "Star-Spangled Banner" at every home athletic event. We take our responsibility for civic education seriously and provide ample opportunities, programs, and activities in support of that mission.

Preparing Young People for a Global Community

Michael McGill
Scarsdale, New York

Over the last two decades, our nation's schools have become increasingly possessed by the mechanics of a flawed and simplistic reform strategy, one that relies on "metrics" to improve a system that never deeply educated large numbers of children in the first place. The federal government formally endorsed "accountability" in 2002 when it passed the so-called No Child Left Behind (NCLB) law. NCLB defined education narrowly, too often reducing it to a scramble for test scores without enough corresponding support. The law was designed so that it would ultimately characterize large numbers of schools as failures. Not surprisingly, many of these were in urban centers and rural areas, serving children whose families were poorer and less well educated.

During this same period, America's schools have faced challenges whose dimensions NCLB does not fully encompass. Students today are graduating into a world where they must participate and compete with others whose abilities have been forged in other systems of education. They need to think clearly, critically, and creatively, to understand themselves in the context of the human experience and the natural universe, and to express themselves intelligently and effectively. The future of our democracy depends on their active contribution.

Alarmingly, international tests, such as those sponsored by the Programme for International Student Assessment (PISA), raise serious questions about whether students from even the best American schools can meet a high world standard. The continuing educational disparity between wealthy and poor, whites and people of color, simply exacerbates the problem.

As the nation begins at last to recognize the need to overcome longstanding economic and racial inequities, many so-called "high-performing" districts have found themselves sidelined, their experience apparently irrelevant to the "real" issues playing out in the cities. These districts, often in the suburbs, continue to succeed according to the usual measures: state tests, SAT scores, AP scores, college admission. This apparent success gives them many reasons just to hunker down and do what they know how to do. Not only are there few evident incentives to change but their own success is actually a disincentive to speak up or to think independently. Why fix what's not broken? Why threaten what's made you good? Why risk criticism or controversy?

The questions, then, for these more favored places are, Will they be satisfied with their apparent success, or will they accept the challenge offered by the emerging international context? Will they remain on the periphery, or will they try to engage more directly in regional and national efforts to define America's educational future? If they choose, they can model an education that prepares students for democracy and an interdependent world, they can develop networks of exemplary practice in cooperation with other districts, and they can educate their communities and leaders in politics and business about the kind of education all Americans deserve.

With this context as background, the Scarsdale Schools embraced an end goal of preparing young people for the global community. As some have observed, this work goes beyond helping students appreciate different cultures or learn more content or even learn content that's more difficult. In addition, it's essential to foster hard-to-teach abilities: a capacity for complex analysis and critical judgment, original and creative thinking, perseverance, and, especially, a desire to learn. By also seeking to impart an ethic of contribution, the district endeavors to graduate people who will make a positive difference in their nation and the world.

How are the schools addressing these priorities? A sample of our actions follows.

- *Literacy:* Of the skills necessary to long-term success, none is more basic than the capacity to read and write effectively. The district has revised its literacy guide, which provides the framework for instruction in grades K–5. Teachers are using the Developmental Reading Assessment (DRA) as a key reading assessment tool. In the coming year, they will continue efforts to improve reading instruction based on student needs identified by the DRA. The district is contracting with Teachers College, Columbia, and other organizations to provide extensive professional development for all elementary classroom teachers as they address the literacy needs of all students.

- *Advanced mathematics:* The future of the world community, the nation, and individual citizens in many ways depends on a high level of mathematical literacy. As a result of improvements in the elementary school math program in recent years, the middle and high schools have been able to accelerate math instruction for students by a full year beyond the curriculum they would traditionally have taken. Ultimately, this gain should enable as many as 80 percent of high school students to take calculus, compared with about 55 percent a decade ago.

In 2008–2009, elementary school faculty began to use the next generation of texts, Singapore Math, for grades K–5. To get ready for this transition, teachers revised and developed a new math curriculum based on the new standards released by the National Council of Teachers of Mathematics in a document titled, "Curriculum Focal Points: A Quest for Coherence."

After a highly successful Scarsdale Math Differentiation Symposium that involved Carole Tomlinson and others, middle school teachers are continuing to develop their ability to address the different aptitudes among students. High school teachers meanwhile will continue to adjust student course groupings in response to individual differences, and an added math teacher position will support efforts to ready the largest number of pupils for calculus.

- *World languages:* Graduates will benefit from and contribute more effectively to the global community if they can speak at least one second language fluently; therefore, the district has begun to offer Spanish instruction in the elementary grades. According to external evaluation, implementation in the primary years has gone well, and we will now begin to offer the language in the intermediate years before finally connecting to and adapting the program in the middle and high schools.

The decision to offer Spanish in grades 1–5 raises questions about how this head start will affect the future of our world language program. Adaptations will be necessary in our middle and high school Spanish classes. Further, we will introduce Mandarin in 2009–2010, with the possibility of teaching Arabic in the future. It's in our students' interest for their schools to sustain a broad and rich program of language offerings, and we will need to look carefully at how best to reap the benefits of early instruction while continuing to promote program breadth.

- *The arts initiative:* Dana Gioia, chair of the National Endowment of the Arts, recently told a Stanford University audience that "the (real) purpose of arts education . . . is to create complete human beings capable of leading successful and productive lives." He added, "If the United States is to compete effectively with the rest of the world [we need the] creativity, ingenuity and innovation" that the arts nurture.

Scarsdale faculty members have engaged in a yearlong review of the arts program as it is and could be. Among the first results was a decision to enhance grade 3 instrumental music offerings. More broadly, faculty have begun to consider how to develop original thinking and creativity purposefully through engagement with the arts by more fully integrating them with academics and by building on existing connections among subjects. Next steps will be to take advantage of a new affiliation with the Lincoln Center Institute and Carnegie Hall education programs.

- *The Capstone Project:* As noted earlier, members of the global community need to be able to ask important questions, to learn independently, and to evaluate the significance of the information they acquire. These are dispositions that should be nurtured early, when children are inherently curious and eager to learn.

Toward that end, each fifth grader in 2006–2007 undertook major research on a topic of his or her interest. Projects ranged from inquiry into solar energy and the origins of flight to the plays of William Shakespeare. Students identified and narrowed a question, found information in libraries and online, applied interview skills, prepared written work, and ultimately made verbal presentations for panels of adults.

Originally an outgrowth of technology initiatives, the Capstone Project became a culminating exercise of the skills and knowledge students had developed in their elementary school years. It is a good example of a rich, well-developed, final assessment of the sort that ought to be the backbone of student performance evaluation. The results of this assessment are available through the student information system in a format that allows professional staff to examine both individual results and patterns of group performance. Most important for many students, however, the Capstone Project was an opportunity to explore a significant area of personal interest, evoking an excitement about learning that is one of the district's most important objectives.

• *The Human Rights Project:* The hallmark of Scarsdale Middle School is its dual emphasis on individual growth and on service to others. Over the past three years, the Human Rights Project has offered students a superb opportunity to learn about human rights issues worldwide and to make a difference.

Furthermore, it is increasingly evident that matters of human rights relate to sustainability concerns. For example, when middle school students constructed a human "pump" to raise funds for potable water retrieval in Africa, they learned that rights abuses often reflect resource shortages. Students also met with Bol Riiny, one of the "lost boys" of Sudan, and learned about the sources of the tragic conflict there: land, water, and grazing rights, among others. These kinds of connections make the larger world more immediate for children who are insulated from the problems of poverty and overt strife in so many ways, and they help students appreciate how privilege confers responsibility.

• *Advanced Topics:* Scarsdale High School has embarked on an ambitious plan to shift away from the Advanced Placement program it introduced in the 1950s and instead develop its own college-level curriculum for highly motivated students, one that emphasizes complex, critical, and creative thinking and self-expression. It will do this by covering challenging material and by encouraging extended inquiries that require students to exercise skill and perseverance.

Art and social studies teachers, in collaboration with counterparts from the university level, spent the summer of 2007 preparing course syllabi, instructional unit plans, and materials. Going forward, they will continue to meet with university teachers to review progress and see how Scarsdale students' work measures up against expectations for first-year college students. Joint committees of faculty and parents will also review progress. Expansion to other subjects will be considered in the coming year. The Advanced Topics endeavor generated considerable community discussion. The faculty is committed to make it an example of a local initiative that will improve learning and enhance students' success in college and in life.

- *Sustainability Initiative:* In 2006–2007, the board of education adopted the long-term objective of reducing the district's carbon emissions in the year 2020 to 10 percent below the 1990 level. This target is bold, especially in view of the significant amount of square footage added to the physical plant since 1990.

The district developed a sustainability plan for the future. The plan is in three parts, involving improvements in the operation of the buildings and grounds and in the educational program, as well as changes in individual behavior. Building on the work begun in 2006–2007 and on a very successful summer leadership program, site-based committees at each school are addressing the long-term district objective through education and conservation.

- *Interdependence Institute:* Since its inception in 2002, this institute has sought to enhance the experience of international students in Scarsdale and to promote connections with the broader world. It has sponsored meetings between teachers and members of the international community as well as films and speakers, and it has more recently affiliated with the East-West Center in Hawaii. Students and teachers have traveled to Southeast Asia; recently, eight students and three teachers were accepted for the Partnership for Youth program in Cambodia, observing and journaling the tribunal that is seeking closure to the suffering that occurred under the Khmer Rouge regime.

Going forward, the institute will continue to assess local curriculum in light of globalization, and it will also provide more academic and social opportunities for international families and students. Additionally, there are plans to extend the relationship with the East-West Center, promote more international teacher exchanges, and develop a school partnership or other connection with schools in China, in addition to existing connections in Spain and France.

More broadly, we in America regularly hear that our public schools fail to meet rigorous international standards. Indeed, as the Scarsdale Board of Education learned from visiting Harvard professor Richard Elmore, the United States is relatively far from the top on tests like those sponsored by PISA.

The PISA examinations are unusual in that they attempt to measure higher-order thinking, and they are quite familiar to many people in other nations. For example, the Japanese are concerned that Finland is now the highest performer in the world, while its own performance has fallen. They are doing their best to evaluate the reasons and to learn from other nations how they can improve. The emerging international context makes such engagement necessary. At the same time, it gives reason for caution. Looking abroad, for example, one quickly becomes aware of the difficulties inherent in academic winnowing systems where students are selected for more and more competitive admission to the next level of education on the basis of national curricula and high-stakes testing. Typically, these systems do what they are designed to do, but with consequences that must be viewed in context. In Japan, for instance, university education is evidently an anticlimax after the hours students spend studying in high school. Meanwhile, there are relatively few second chances for young people who, in an American system, would have more chances.

Different systems rest on different assumptions, which often lead to somewhat different objectives. While understanding that we here in America have room for growth but that there is no one best method of educating the young, our schools must strive to learn from others and at the same time nurture the ingenuity, the intellectual flexibility, the originality of thought, and the other strengths that have historically proven so important to our citizens, our nation, and the world.

High-performing school districts have a valuable part to play in this process. As noted at the outset, however, they face a dilemma. Because of their resources and the advantages their students already possess when they arrive at the schoolhouse door, these schools are easily dismissed as atypical and too far removed from the real problems of real schools to have anything important to say to public education at large. Their direct access to resources such as a Dr. Elmore or a Dr. Tomlinson, for example, can be a reason to discount any contribution they might try to make.

Nonetheless, the things that make high-performing school districts successful are the same things that make any school good: a clear and common sense of mission; curious, motivated students; well-educated and eager teachers; high standards; appropriate resources.

How do successful schools promote these essentials? The following are some examples, in no special order:

- Professionals are familiar with pupil work that meets high international standards. They aim to produce work of this quality.
- Professional staff are well educated and think well; they have personally experienced quality teaching and learning in their own schooling.
- Governing boards regularly evaluate their work to ensure a focus on educational ends as opposed to over involvement with means.
- Students participate in classes and work on assignments that combine important academic content with their personal interests, where possible.
- Professional staff members participate in continuing education and see themselves as learners every day throughout their careers.
- A critical mass of board members, administrators, teachers, parents, and students believe that their common purpose is to learn.
- Teachers help students understand why topics and issues are important, and how they relate to the students' own experience.
- Professionals use varied measures to assess student performance. Standardized testing is judicious and as noninvasive as possible.

- Boards and top leadership understand their respective roles, work well together, and provide stable, long-term direction for schools.
- Classes and student loads are small enough for teachers to know how their pupils think and to understand them as individuals.
- Students learn not only important skills and knowledge but also to think analytically, independently, and originally about significant content.
- Each student knows, trusts, and is known well by at least one adult in the school.
- Students have multiple opportunities to involve themselves in out-of-class activities that will connect them to the school.
- Professionals have time and opportunity to share knowledge and to work collaboratively so that they build on each other's efforts.
- The school is a safe place where people respect one another and actively collaborate for the common good.
- Students and professional staff have opportunities to exercise academic initiative and creativity. These lend energy and enthusiasm to learning.

Many of these characteristics depend less on funding and more on the vision, goodwill, determination, and endurance of leaders at every level: governing boards, superintendents, principals, and teachers. Some do require a level of resource that is currently unavailable in too many schools. While money is not sufficient to produce educational quality, it is necessary, especially for developing a highly educated and effective teaching force and for supporting student-teacher ratios low enough for professionals to understand and respond effectively to their children's thinking.

Once upon a time, the main goals of public schooling were to teach the mechanics of reading, writing, and arithmetic, to homogenize a diverse population, and to produce workers for the factory floor. In those days, it was enough for a teacher to present material to groups of thirty or more children and to expect them—or enough of them—to grasp enough of what was taught so that they could function in an economy much different from today's and in a different, more limited world.

Today, successful participation and contribution rely more and more on abstract, critical, and original thinking; the capacity to use what one knows to solve unfamiliar problems; and the ability to apply judgment in complex, often unclear situations. These kinds of aptitudes develop through deep engagement with important subject matter in the humanities and sciences. And that kind of engagement is the product of a close encounter of minds—the teacher's and the student's.

What the high-performing districts have to say to the rest of education is that quality schools are sometimes highly innovative and sometimes places of well-tried practice but that what matters most is what has always mattered: the quality of the people, the quality of their thinking, and the quality of relationships. Correspondingly, leadership in these places is the act of engaging people with these issues, of sponsoring learning communities that are models of excellence, of establishing networks of quality to link schools together, and of reaching out to educate communities and leaders in fields such as business and politics so that they will advocate for policies most apt to foster the public schools our republic requires.

Ten Strengths of Resilient Superintendents in Changing Times

Jerry L. Patterson
Birmingham, Alabama

Diane E. Reed
Rochester, New York

For the past several years, we have been heavily involved in research to better understand the concept of leader resilience and to develop strategies that strengthen the resilience of superintendents and other leaders. In this paper, we outline concrete steps to take to help you become a more resilient leader.

In a sentence, resilience is the demonstrated ability to recover, learn from, and grow stronger when confronted with chronic or crisis adversity. Resilience is not a short-term phenomenon. Leaders don't wake up in the morning resilient and go to bed nonresilient. They may feel tired, discouraged, optimistic, or drained, but resilience doesn't fluctuate like the weather or stock market. In the words of Paul Houston, former executive director of the American Association of School Administrators, "If you have a short-term view, it is very hard to be resilient, because in the short term things are going to happen that aren't good. A long-term view makes it almost impossible not to be resilient, because this too shall pass" (Patterson & Kelleher, 2005, p. 20). Resilience is thus strengthened (or diminished) over time.

Based on our extensive study of the research and best practices of resilient superintendents, we have identified ten strengths that emerge as crucial in supporting effective leadership during tough times. Below we briefly describe those strengths and give concrete examples of how resilient superintendents have applied them in their leadership roles.

STRENGTH: MAINTAIN AN OPTIMISTIC PERSPECTIVE ABOUT FUTURE POSSIBILITIES

We realize that it is extremely challenging for superintendents to stay positive when they are bombarded by so many negative circumstances. There are days when you are sad, disappointed, and discouraged. Resilient superintendents acknowledge these short-term setbacks and, at the same time, keep "their eyes on the prize."

A superintendent in a fast-growing district led the charge to pass a community referendum on building a new high school and two new elementary schools to accommodate the rapid increase in enrollment. For the first time in twenty years, the community voted down the referendum proposal, and the superintendent felt personally responsible for the defeat. Demonstrating an optimistic perspective, the superintendent asked the question, "How can we find common ground with the community and take a small step toward relieving our overcrowded conditions?" The superintendent concluded that the community would most likely support the two elementary schools because overcrowding was visibly a serious concern. So a subsequent referendum was presented just for the elementary schools, and the community resoundingly supported the proposal. Two years later, when high school enrollments were spilling over into portable trailers, the community passed a referendum to build a new high school.

Optimism is thus a mindset that shapes how leaders think about their roles in making a difference. Other strategies to help strengthen your leadership resilience in the area of optimism include:

- Always find a way to have a positive influence, however small, in making good things happen.

- Focus your leadership energy on the opportunities, not the obstacles, but don't discount the importance of the obstacles.
- Maintain a respectful sense of humor in the face of adversity.

STRENGTH: WORK HARD TO DEVELOP A COMPREHENSIVE PICTURE OF REALITY WHEN FACED WITH ADVERSITY

Whereas optimism is about future possibilities, this strength is about the "here and now." Resilient superintendents gather all the facts and perspectives, from multiple and diverse perspectives, so they can make the best decisions possible under fire. This means that you seek out the bad news as well as the good news, but you don't dwell on the bad news.

One superintendent was in the midst of recruiting for an assistant superintendent. The superintendent recalled a principal in a neighboring district who had a deserved reputation for "calling it like it is," even when the principal's perspective was not popular with her supervisor. The superintendent deliberately sought out the principal and invited her to apply for the assistant superintendent position. She was ultimately hired for the position. Later, the superintendent informed her,

> One of the reasons I hired you is that you have the courage to offer your perspective on what is really going on around here, even when it is not a perspective shared by others. As hard as it will be for me at times when you take issue with my perspective, both I and the district value your perspective.

The superintendent demonstrated resilience by surrounding himself with other leaders who would contribute to a comprehensive understanding of reality.

Other indicators of resilience within the category of understanding reality are:

- Accept the reality that adversity typically is both inevitable and unexpected.
- Realize that sometimes reality poses upper limits on what can actually be accomplished.
- Find ways to focus on the positive aspects of adverse circumstances to balance the negative aspects.

STRENGTH: SUSTAIN A STRONG SUPPORT BASE

When you think of strong leaders who withstand the storms of adversity, you typically think of tough-minded, courageous individuals standing tall and, usually, alone. Our research shows that the "Lone Ranger" may work in the short run. There are many examples of superintendents who make the tough calls and live to tell about it. Remember, though, that resilience isn't about the short run. Over the long haul, leading in the face of adversity takes its toll. As Patterson documented in his AASA book *The Anguish of Leadership* (2000), when leaders repeatedly make courageous decisions, they put rocks in their pockets. Over time, the cumulative weight of the rocks can drown you. To help prevent the long-term toll of leading in the face of adversity, superintendents need somewhere to turn for support as well as advice.

Several years ago, a group of suburban superintendents in the Boston area decided to contract the services of a psychologist to periodically meet with them and guide them through emotional discussions about life as a superintendent. The superintendents involved were quick to point to the value of being able to have professional support available, and they weren't embarrassed to ask for it.

Support can take various forms, including:

- Reach out to build trusting relationships with those you can confide in.
- Seek to learn from the experiences of others who successfully faced similar circumstances.
- Actively share with your support base your small wins along the road to recovery from adversity.

STRENGTH: STAY CENTERED ON CORE VALUES WHEN ADVERSITY STRIKES

Superintendents tell us that, among all of the important resilience strengths that they draw on in tough times, being value driven is the number one priority on their list. It's rather easy and straightforward to be value driven during so-called normal times. It gets a lot harder to be clear and unwavering on what matters most when you feel the pressure of competing forces borne out of adversity.

For instance, suppose your district is faced with making severe budget cuts in a short period of time. You decide to hold a series of public forums to get feedback and perspectives on how to approach these tough decisions. Not surprisingly, the athletic booster group organizes a blitzkrieg by bombarding the school board with personal phone calls and by dominating the forums with carefully calculated speeches arguing that athletics gives the community a strong sense of identity. Further, the coaches organize their teams to attend the public forums, all decked out in their uniforms displaying the school colors. And they occupy the first three rows in the forum.

Now you are faced with the competing values of listening to diverse perspectives, which you asked for, versus values that focus on student learning. Between these competing values, where do you land? As we elaborate later, resilience in large part is about making the courageous decisions based on your own hierarchy of values, even when your values don't align with the most important values of many members of the community, or perhaps even the school board.

The most resilient superintendents apply value-driven strategies such as:

- Don't let opposing forces distort your vision about what matters most to you among competing values.
- Work hard to consistently clarify for yourself and publicly articulate for others your core values.
- Always rely on strongly held moral or ethical principles to guide you through adversity.

STRENGTH: ACCEPT PERSONAL RESPONSIBILITY FOR MAKING AND IMPLEMENTING TOUGH DECISIONS IN THE FACE OF THE STORM

All of us will be quick to agree that effective leaders need to be accountable for their actions. But this is easier said than done. When superintendents make decisions that turn out, in hindsight, to be unwise, or when superintendents act impulsively without appropriate reflection, the results send us to the nearest fallout shelter.

A superintendent in a large metropolitan school district decided to recommend to the school board that each student be provided free laptops to use in the classroom. The recommendation made national news long before the school board had been informed about it. Not surprisingly, school board members received phone calls asking them what they thought of the plan and challenging them to show how such a major purchase, especially in light of severe budget problems, was going to have a direct impact on instruction. In summary, the board was caught off guard because the superintendent had trumpeted the announcement to everyone but the board.

At the next regularly scheduled board meeting, the superintendent began by apologizing to the board for his short-sighted action. He acknowledged that the plan should first have been presented to the board, not to the rest of the world. He also accepted personal responsibility for his mistake and pledged not to let it happen in the future.

Even superintendents are human, and we all make mistakes. When these things happen (hopefully very rarely), we can rebuild trust by pointing out how we messed up and issuing assurances that it won't happen again. Then, of course, we need to walk our talk. Other strategies that superintendents can use to strengthen their resilience in the area of personal responsibility include:

- Stay cognizant of the fact that when you decide *not* to take action in the face of adversity you must also assume personal accountability for that action.
- Accept accountability for the long-term organizational impact of any tough leadership decisions you make.
- Accept responsibility for making needed changes *personally* in those cases where you contributed to the adversity.

STRENGTH: MAINTAIN A CONFIDENT PRESENCE AS A LEADER IN THE MIDST OF ADVERSITY

Efficacy is our sense that we are effective in the world. It describes our belief that we can solve the problems we are likely to experience in the superintendency and our faith in our ability to succeed.

A superintendent, during the first week of the school year, received word that there had been a tragic accident associated with a school field trip. Three students and a teacher had lost their lives. The superintendent immediately took charge of the situation and called the crisis team together to follow the plan they had developed and practiced in case of just such an event. They quickly put into action internal and external communications and dealt with the victims' families, the student body, staff, and community at-large. Getting all the stakeholders through a tragedy of this magnitude generally strengthens one's personal efficacy.

Efficacy thus refers to your beliefs about your capacity to overcome a life storm and galvanize people for collective action. Other strategies to help strengthen your leadership resilience in the area of efficacy include:

- Always take a deliberate, step-by-step approach to overcome adversity.
- Always be confident that you can learn from the adversity to help you be stronger in the future.
- Offset any relative leadership weakness you have in an area by turning to others who have strength in that area.

STRENGTH: FULLY ENGAGE THROUGH PERSISTENCE

Successful school leaders understand the importance of perseverance. A leader needs to have a huge amount of tenacity because it makes up for the times when things are not working out the way you want, for when people are disgruntled, or for when people don't share your vision.

Several years ago, a suburban superintendent in Upstate New York implemented a middle school one-on-one laptop initiative for students in grades 6–8. The PTA escalated pressure to derail the initiative because its members did not want their children to have access to games, instant messaging, and the possibility of unsafe contacts on the Internet. The central strategy of the group was to wear the superintendent down with ridiculous demands. But the superintendent persevered. The district worked with the parents to offer training to students and their families on how to put safeguards in place. Parents who wanted their child to bring the laptop home had to give their permission. Parents were thus given the option of having their children use the laptop only in school during the day and leaving it there.

The superintendent kept the focus on integrating technology into teaching and learning while still listening to the parents' concerns, validating their fears, and working out viable alternatives, thus keeping the program going.

To successfully persist over the long haul, a superintendent must maintain and manage his or her energy by keeping motivation and determination high and staying fully engaged. Do not let disruptive forces and other distractions interfere with staying focused on the most important goals and tasks. Other strategies that superintendents can use to strengthen their resilience in the area of perseverance include:

- Always maintain a steady, concentrated focus on the most important priorities amid adversity until success is attained.
- Do not let adversity in one aspect of your life have a long-term impact on the resilience in other parts of your life.
- Do not let disruptive forces and other distractions interfere with keeping the focus on important goals and tasks.

STRENGTH: REMAIN FLEXIBLE IN TIMES OF STRESS AND PRESSURE

Effective superintendents recognize that the complexity of their job means that mistakes are inevitable. They have learned to rebound. What is more, they value the personal flexibility that allows them to recover quickly from setbacks.

As a superintendent publicly stated his goals for the year, he noticed the looks on the board members' faces and realized that he had not informed them in advance of his remarks so that they could be prepared and not surprised. The superintendent immediately realized he had made a mistake by not communicating upfront with the board of education. The important point is not that he had failed to communicate but, instead, how quickly he recovered. The superintendent immediately went back to the board and acknowledged that he had made a mistake. He believed in what he was doing, but his capacity to get it done would be greatly diminished without their support. He asked for support after the fact, and fortunately, they gave it to him; but he learned to make every effort not to put them in that predicament again.

Other indicators of resilience within the category of flexibility are:

- Adjust your expectations about what is possible based on what you have learned about the reality of the current situation.
- Put your mistakes in perspective and move beyond them.
- Always search for various workable strategies to achieve positive results in a difficult situation.

STRENGTH: MAINTAIN PHYSICAL AND EMOTIONAL WELL-BEING

Resilient superintendents demonstrate an overall strength of physical and emotional well-being while effectively carrying out their leadership role. They pay attention to their personal health factors and adjust their behavior accordingly.

A veteran superintendent told us, with some embarrassment, that he was not able to monitor his own physical health factors. His "circuitry" was wired such that he would drive himself to exhaustion. So he turned to his wife to serve as monitor and enforcer, and he listened to her when she told him that the telltale signs were pointing to another physical collapse. When she saw the train wreck about to happen, she would arrange a long weekend getaway for the two of them and tell him to set aside those dates because she had planned an outing for them. It worked! He would come back from the escape with replenished physical energy.

Taking care of one's self, both physically and emotionally, can take other forms, including:

- Do not let adverse circumstances that inevitably happen disrupt your long-term focus on maintaining a healthy lifestyle.
- Create time to replenish your emotional energy.
- Find healthy ways to channel physical energy as a stress reliever.

STRENGTH: BE A COURAGEOUS DECISION MAKER

Leaders shape culture. It is their responsibility to change it. During tough times the pressure on leaders is even greater. Larry Lezotte (1991) reflected on leaders with whom he has worked during times of adversity by noting the challenge of growing cultural values. He commented that at a critical point the responsibility rests with the leader. Too often, when things change, cultural roots need to deepen to take firm hold. A female superintendent in a small rural setting was faced with a most difficult situation. The main pride of this small town was their high school football team. The team for many years in a row had been the state champions. At the last game of an undefeated season, a serious fight occurred wherein, upon investigation, the lead football players of the district ferociously attacked two players from the opposing team. The two students were taken to the hospital with broken bones. The superintendent followed appropriate disciplinary actions and worked cooperatively with law enforcement officers. Parents pressed charges, and in the end, the leading senior football player who had had a full scholarship to a Division I school lost his scholarship. The entire community rallied and put extreme pressure on the board of education to overrule the superintendent. The core values of teaching, learning, and ethical behavior were being challenged because this community's core value had been football and winning the coveted state championship. The superintendent, under extreme pressure, stayed the course. At the next board election, the community elected two board members who ran on the platform of removing the superintendent. She saw the handwriting on the wall and applied and accepted a superintendency in another community that better matched her core values.

This superintendent did what was right and stood by her decision. Yet, over time, she did a reality check and, as a realistic optimist, realized that she needed to take control and move to a place where her core values matched that of the community and district.

The most resilient superintendents apply courageous decision-making strategies such as:

- Seek out perspectives that differ significantly from yours so you can make the most informed decisions possible.
- Be able to make principled decisions that, at times, are contrary to respected advice by others.
- Take prompt, principled action in emergency situations demanding immediate response.

We have identified ten strengths of superintendents who demonstrate the ability to recover, learn from, and grow stronger when confronted with chronic or crisis adversity. We have provided brief vignettes of superintendents who applied these strengths in real-life situations. Our hope is that you, too, will apply these strengths to help you through the storms you confront in the superintendency and that you emerge on the other side of the storm stronger than ever.

SUMMARY

Changing Times Research

Meet student needs, value equity over equality, support high achievement for every student, acknowledge accountability for all, implement culturally responsive leadership, respect diversity.

Most Effective Practices for Changing Times

- Be creative
- Meet the needs of underserved students
- Partner with community colleges
- Measure success differently from the past
- Serve others
- Infuse the curriculum with a global emphasis
- Be optimistic
- Stay centered on core values
- Adopt curricula for the changing times
- Prepare young people for a global community

CHANGING TIMES REFLECTION

1. How have the demographics of your district changed within the past ten years? five years?

2. What are you doing to acknowledge the changing demographics in your district?

3. In what ways does your leadership emphasize cultural proficiency?

4. What are you doing to help others in your district become more culturally proficient?

5. Where are you weak in these areas?

6. Write a prescription for improvement for you to become more focused on educating students in these changing times.

7. What ideas in this chapter were the most important for your district?

8. How can you implement or revise ideas in this chapter to improve your district?

ADDITIONAL RESOURCES

Bol Riiny—"lost boy" of Sudan. http://www.bard.edu/news/releases/pr/fstory.php?id=1418

Developmental Reading Assessment (DRA). http://plgcatalog.pearson.com/program_multiple.cfm?site_id=2&program_id+200&searchtype+Title&searchTerm=dra

Human Rights Project. http://www.hrproject.org

Programme for International Student Assessment (PISA). http://www.pisa.oecd.org

Singapore Math. http://www.singaporemath.com

CHAPTER FIVE

School Reform

Many schools resist change while others avidly seek it. If we do not want our schools to atrophy and die, we need educational leaders who can bring about progress by daring to be change managers.

—Jon Andreas

Your success as a leader who gets the most from people won't depend upon your title, your degrees, or your previous experience. It won't be the result of how much you know, how hard you work, what long hours you keep, or anything you say. It will rest almost totally on the way you treat people.

—Robert Ramsey

There is an increasing awareness of the need for an educated populace that has led to concerted efforts to improve schools around the world. However, bringing about reform in a school district is a challenge, and not all efforts have resulted in improved student achievement (Elmore, 2000). Superintendents, though, are not easily discouraged given their passion to bring about school reform. As an example, in 2007, the American Association of School Administrators (AASA) brought together the 2007 Superintendent of the Year winners and representatives from the Charles Stewart Mott Foundation (C.S. Mott Foundation) and the Forum for Youth Investment (FYI) (American Association of School Administrators, 2008). This group identified five avenues for creating a new learning system: (1) reframe the challenge, (2) re-envision the structures, (3) redefine goals, (4) recalibrate the learning environments, and (5) redefine leadership. Much of the discussion resonated with the notion of changing the conversation for school reform to be less about schools and more about meeting the needs of children.

There is increasingly clear evidence in the school reform research that long-term benefits accrue to schools and students when there are professional learning opportunities and collaborative creative communities of practice (S. Harris, 2005c). Other literature has found that effective leaders exert a powerful influence on student achievement (Waters & Marzano, 2006). As the role of the superintendent has become more focused on young people, major initiatives in today's school reform efforts often identify the superintendent as the official instructional leader of the school district. Consistent with this trend, at a recent AASA meeting of recognized school leaders, superintendents identified seven concrete strategies for creating seamless learning experiences for each student. These include:

1. value and give credit to learning experiences that occur in and out of the classroom;

2. involve school staff throughout the school system—during the school day and after school hours;

3. extend credit for experience, not just class time;

4. embed learning in real-life situations in and out of school;

5. offer college credit while in high school;

6. provide access to technology; and

7. ensure vertical articulation. (American Association of School Administrators, 2008, p. 9)

There is little doubt that superintendents who implement and sustain positive school reform efforts must meet Senge's (1990) challenge to help organizations adapt to an environment of accelerated change. For example, one barrier to effective school reform pointed out by Kelleher and Van Der Bogert (2006) is that the typical tenure of a superintendent is approximately six to seven years, yet many veteran teachers have been in communities for twenty-five years or more. These individuals have seen reform initiatives come and go for a variety of reasons, leading to skepticism on their part about the possibility of true reform. Superintendents, however, are responsible for leading individuals within the organization to enlarge their capabilities and thus participate in the shaping of their own futures. The entire organization must become involved in a continuous process of learning, renewal, and improvement for school reform efforts to be successful. As stated so eloquently by Yogi Berra, "Sometimes change means doing things different" (quoted in Blaydes, 2003, p. 83).

The superintendent is the change agent for school reform; however, to be effective, the people within the organization must buy into the changes needed since they are the ones who will (or will not) carry out reform implementation successfully. Consequently, people are the most important assets within the school district.

In the articles that follow, award-winning superintendents share their responses to the mandate for superintendents to lead school reform efforts. I organized these selections into the following categories: achievement gap challenges, specific strategies for school reform, and overcoming barriers to school reform. Brenda Dietrich considers strategies to reduce the achievement gap, while Robert Olsen describes curricular reforms in his district that led to increased achievement for special education students and limited English proficient students. Chuck Holt describes how his district closed the achievement gap through faculty training.

George Goens describes a specific school reform strategy that utilizes an educational summit for evaluating areas where the district needs to improve. Brenda Dietrich then shares how research leads to school reform, and Chuck Holt discusses evaluating school programs. To overcome school reform barriers, George Goens suggests that leaders should ask the important question: What doesn't make sense? Additional barriers to overcoming school reform are organizational in nature, as identified by Brenda Dietrich and Robert Olsen.

The Achievement Gap: What Are WE Going to Do About It?

Brenda Dietrich
Topeka, Kansas

Although our district is high achieving overall and considered an affluent suburban district of highly educated professionals, we have pockets of poverty and demographic groups in the community and school attendance areas where achievement gaps have not been addressed adequately in the past. When we disaggregated our test data on state assessments, low performance in these groups became brutal facts that we could no longer ignore. We obviously had groups of students in the district who were not performing at appropriate levels in reading and math. It was thus very clear that we had a noticeable achievement gap among our subgroups, as identified by NCLB.

Even though I am not a great fan of NCLB, this was a wake-up call for certain segments in the community who felt the district was doing so well we needn't concern ourselves with AYP. We always were above the state and national averages on the SATs and ACTs. In 2008 we were the only district in Shawnee County to have National Merit finalists, and we had not one, but four! Ninety percent of our students were above proficiency levels in reading and math, but we needed to ask ourselves, "What about the kids who were not?" We had students who were not achieving at appropriate levels, and we needed to have a plan that addressed what we were going to do about it. The conversation and solutions could not focus on external issues or on what parents were going to do. Nor could we blame socioeconomic status or use the excuse that perhaps students did not go to a quality preschool. The fact was, these students were ours. What were *we* going to do? We also had to analyze and quantify the kinds of skill gaps we were seeing.

The first step we took in developing a plan to address the achievement gap was to look at the district from a "systems" perspective. If we were to focus on teaching and learning, then our curriculum "house" had to be in order. We needed to align our curriculum to the state standards, and we needed to be able to guarantee to our community that our curriculum was consistently taught throughout the district, even though there are ten different buildings.

There are three legs to a viable curriculum: what is tested, what is taught, and what is written. All three areas must be determined collaboratively, written up with specificity and clarity, approved by the board of education, and implemented throughout all classrooms in the district. We contracted with Phi Delta Kappa to conduct an onsite audit four years ago. From that experience and the auditor's recommendations, we were forced to take a very hard, thorough look at our curriculum. It was clear that we weren't aligned internally, either horizontally or vertically, and certainly not to state standards. Our teachers and curriculum coordinators worked diligently for three years to develop an aligned curriculum. The beauty of the process could be seen from day one when we observed teachers working in committees, engaging in professional dialog with one another, and working collaboratively to develop a really strong and viable curriculum. Now when we take state assessments, we can collect student data and disaggregate it, easily identify groups of students not performing on level, develop strategies, and provide interventions. We also now conduct early warning assessments tied directly to state assessments. Teachers developed common assessments that are given to second to tenth graders several times a year. The early warning assessments function like a dipstick. They are a quick check that indicates what skills or portions of curriculum content areas have been mastered by students and what has not. This check allows teachers to adjust instruction in the classroom by regrouping students based on skill needs.

We have been able to develop a mastery and essential curriculum that sits at the center of a bull's-eye. We actually use a color-coded bull's-eye to visually represent the way we prioritize and identify Kansas curricular standards that must be taught to mastery and are a district priority in the local curriculum. All staff must teach the mastery and essential curriculum, and all staff members have participated in identifying those curriculum elements. This curricula was nothing we dictated at all. It was designed by teachers in grade-level meetings based on which state standards were tested and should be taught at that grade level. Now we have a guaranteed curriculum that sits at the center of the bull's-eye, and that curriculum is what we target in those early warning assessments. This process offers a way to track how well students are doing. If they are not doing well, we step back, regroup, and reteach.

Information gained from early warning assessments thus helps direct instruction and focuses data-driven decision making. The assessment scores ensure that we are all focused on the same goals and that students are achieving at their highest levels. When we looked at the data and saw that there were groups of kids that needed support, we located resources and provided interventions for them at the earliest point in their educational progress. For example, we hired literacy coaches at the primary level. Literacy coaches work directly with students to tutor them in phonics and reading and ensure they have a strong foundation in literacy skills. We also offer additional instructional opportunities either before or after school and intensive assistance in utilizing resources in the classroom, and we have software programs such as Success Maker and Waterford that offer additional opportunities for students to master the indicators.

We use instruments other than our early warning assessments, such as the DIBELS test in K–1, several times a year. The district moved slowly at first because collaboration and conversation around teaching and learning were new avenues for us to explore with our staff and because we were asking staff to use a new model to analyze student data and provide just-in-time interventions. We built collaboration time into the elementary school schedule by adding art as a specials time with music and P.E. Our goal was to create professional learning communities (PLCs) that answered DuFour and colleagues' (DuFour, DuFour, Eaker, & Karhanek, 2004) questions about student learning. What is it we expect students to learn? How will we know when they have learned the material? How will we respond when they don't learn? How will we respond when they already know it? At first our teachers weren't sure how to function in a PLC and how to address issues surrounding skill gaps. We asked them to use their collaboration time to create common assessments and to answer DuFour and colleagues' questions about all students. They accomplished a tremendous amount of work over the past three years, and it was not always an easy task for them. They now see, however, that the aligned curriculum (mastery curriculum) makes so much sense in language arts and math that they want to work on science and social studies.

The final manifestation of what we have been engaged in as a "system" is the strong belief that everyone is accountable for every student on our school campuses. We achieved this without preaching it or demanding it or threatening consequences if someone did not fall into step. Because we allowed teachers to learn and grow and work collaboratively toward common goals, they came to that realization themselves. To me, the spread of that feeling of responsibility is the most positive change we have ever implemented in our district and a significant strategy that has allowed us to make sustained and substantive improvements in the district and in student learning.

Achievement Gap
Challenges: Special Education and LEP

Robert Olsen
Sturgis, Michigan

In Sturgis, the greatest achievement gaps exist with special education students and students with limited English proficiency (LEP). This is what we are doing to close the achievement gap:

- With special education students, we have been reviewing and aligning the curriculum with the appropriate general education courses.
- We have provided materials to help teachers better meet the standards that we have established. In addition, we are training our teachers in effective strategies to help students achieve.
- We are providing some clerical support to those teachers to offset the paperwork demands so that teachers are able to focus their efforts where it counts—*with kids.*
- During the school year, we offer extended day learning opportunities for all students; the program is staffed by teachers, paraprofessionals, and volunteers.
- All students, especially those determined to be at risk, have the opportunity to take summer school enrichment and remediation programs.

We have experienced a tremendous demographic shift in our community over the past ten years. Although we have been blessed with significant growth in enrollment, we are challenged by the sheer numbers of Spanish-speaking students. The following additional measures have been taken for our LEP students:

- K–5 teachers are reading a great book, *Classroom Instruction That Works*. Teachers are then discussing the book as a professional learning community during their staff meetings. This professional development is being led by principals and lead teachers.
- We provide support to K–2 LEP students with educational assistants (paraprofessionals) during the school day.
- In grades 3–5, we provide additional ESL support with educational assistants in before-school and after-school sessions that meet every school day. In grades 6–12, students receive direct instruction from an ESL teacher, along with instruction in other classes that is both bilingual and immersive.

Closing the Achievement Gap

Chuck Holt
Lexington, Texas

In my view, this issue of closing the achievement gap may be the number one topic in Texas education today. There are currently more conferences and programs available in this area than ever before. When we look at the Texas accountability system, however, it is easy to see why. The way in which demographic populations are measured drives the ratings of many districts and campuses. It must be remembered that a campus or district rating is established by its lowest group measurement (often TAKS [Texas Assessment of Knowledge and Skills] scores in Texas). In Texas, where economically disadvantaged students are treated as a subpopulation, there is an adage that most campus and district ratings can be determined by zip code. In other words, if you know a campus zip code, it is easy to determine the poverty level, which, in turn, correlates highly with student success on standardized tests. I believe that Fenwick English has proposed this idea on a national basis, also. I know some research in Texas has been done related to this correlation.

Our district has decided to take on this challenge directly. We recently sent all academic department heads to the state Closing the Achievement Gap conference in Austin. From this nationally prominent list of speakers, we learned that we must address the culture of the school as much as the academic opportunities for minority and poor students. First, we have set about retraining our faculty to think differently about school culture. We have provided training titled "40 Developmental Assets" to every faculty member at the high school. Another piece of the puzzle fell into place when our district was named one of the twelve recipients of a Texas High School Redesign and Restructuring grant program. Our primary goal in writing this grant request was to bring all student groups to the same participation and success levels as the white, noneconomically disadvantaged students. For example, all faculty members have committed to thirty measurable goals for minority and poor students. The most challenging of these goals specifically targets these populations for participation in programs such as AP and dual-credit coursework. Within two years, their participation rate is planned to be at the same rate as that of white, middle-class students. This goal will require the district, faculty, and staff to create real and meaningful changes in existing programs to encourage and welcome these students. Formative assessment of these changes will be made by *outside* evaluators as part of the School Enhancement Process. Although this extensive grant addresses many areas, including instructional practices, professional development, curriculum issues, and so on, the goal of closing the achievement gaps is what drives every component.

School Reform Strategy: Dropout Recovery

Daniel King
Pharr, Texas

More than 200 students in our district failed to get their diploma yet hung in there for the four years of high school. I felt we should be able to find those students and help them graduate. We thought about bringing them back into the large, comprehensive high school, but the school was already struggling with AYP and other issues and my feeling was that it wouldn't be a particularly effective strategy. I have learned over the years that, when students only need to pass the TAKS (state achievement test), it's very hard to convince them to go back to school; they convince themselves that they can just take a couple of tutorial sessions and then show up on the test day. Getting them to come to school regularly so they can get the help they need is a challenge. With that challenge in mind, we designed our College, Career, and Technology Academy. We worked with the local community college and, almost overnight, we went from having just an idea to opening a school. In a matter of two weeks we had advertised and hired a principal, the principal had hired teachers, and everything had fallen into place. There was an old Wal-Mart building in town being used for workforce development. It had some vacant rooms that we leased because we wanted a different setting, away from the high school. When these kids started at this campus, we treated them more like college kids, even though some had discipline and attendance issues. Most of these students also had serious life issues.

The community college agreed to work with us to set up a program, and we proceeded to go out into the community to find students who had failed to graduate. When we found them, the message we put out to them was, "You did not get a high school diploma, you did not graduate, but you can start college today." Our idea was that, in this new school environment, we could work with students on TAKS and, at the same time, help them get rolling on a career path and on college coursework. The community college had a course called College Success already developed for incoming freshmen with challenges. This course was like a college orientation/study skills course. We started all of our students in that course, together with whatever area they were deficient in on TAKS or a needed credit area, and hence got them back in school. We designed the program with students in mind who would probably already be working or looking for work and getting married, and we started having them come to school four hours a day, which is enough in Texas for ADA credit. We ran split sessions—8–12 and 12:30–4:30— a cost-effective way to use teachers and administrators.

We enrolled 223 students, and they started in late September. After the mandated state TAKS test in October, we gave them career assessments. We worked with the community college to set up mini-mester courses for students who needed only to pass the TAKS. Some students needed very minimal credits so also took the mini-mester course offerings, which included medical technology, welding, computer courses, and others. We had 49 students graduate in December, and most of those graduates had at least four college credits already. Of the 49 graduates, 26 continued on with college work after graduation. When people come to visit our campus, we show a video of this high school graduation, and it is very emotional to watch. Most of these kids, based on the history of this district, would have never gone back to school, and now they have an opportunity to finish high school and to continue with college.

Every semester we run a new recruiting campaign to bring students who have left the system back into this program. We graduated over 50 students in May 2008. These are mostly kids who were just falling through the cracks. We focus on students who need three credits or less and/or the TAKS test. If students need a whole year of work, we feel a regular high school or another alternative high school would work better and be a more appropriate setting for them. The county judge was so excited about this program that he had us set up a workshop, and every superintendent in the area was invited to come hear about it.

We intentionally designed this campus to meet the kids' needs instead of making kids fit the campus. For this reason, we utilized a different schedule. We are open to night courses, but so far, surprisingly, there hasn't been much interest in them; but we could run that evening shift if the need arises. We also applied for a waiver for flex school accounting so that we can count cumulative hours for attendance. If a student can't come on Monday but can be there Tuesday for two sessions, he or she can still get credit. We don't do this wholesale, but when a young person can't maintain a regular schedule, we deal with it individually and set that student on flex attendance accounting.

We partnered with South Texas College and with the local workforce solutions/development board to help us with recruiting and setting up assessments for career interests. These partnerships also helped us with funding for childcare, along with a grant we received. Offering childcare has been a big challenge, but through the use of those workforce development/grant funds, the program has been successful. We did, however, run out of funds and had to use local money, asking students with young children to contract with daycare providers to take care of the children while they were in school.

Visitors have come to see what we have done, and, I think, they actually overstudy our program. They might come back three times, still trying to figure out whether they can do the same thing next year or the following year. But this is not rocket science; it's common sense, and it's looking at students and identifying their needs. When I presented this idea to the district administration and the board, there were 100 questions. I said I didn't have all the answers, but we were just going to do it; it was unacceptable not to because we were losing kids every semester. We had to implement a program for them. My advice to others is to get it rolling, be flexible, and adjust the design as you go.

We began with determining how close students were to graduating. Counselors went through student files from the senior classes and created two lists: those who did not graduate and those who needed just three credits or less or the TAKS test. When students needed as many as five credits, we placed them in the regular alternative school. When they were down to needing just three credits, we let them transfer to this school.

If every year 200–300 kids leave school without a high school diploma, imagine the impact on our economy and community. And the way we are running this school is fairly cost-effective. Texas House Bill 1137, which discusses funding of schools and attendance, states that schools can receive regular ADA funding for young people up to age twenty-five to help them get a high school diploma. This led us to add a new component to the College, Career, and Technology Academy. In January 2008, we opened our doors to students from prior classes who were unable to receive their high school diploma and were not yet twenty-five years of age. Fourteen students responded and enrolled. This opportunity will be life changing for these young people. Partnerships with colleges, community colleges, workforce agencies, and school districts across the nation could make a dramatic impact on this eighteen- to twenty-five-year-old age group.

School Reform Strategy: Educational Summit for Evaluation

George A. Goens
Litchfield, Connecticut

Successful organizations have integrity and credibility. Credibility and integrity go hand in hand; an organization cannot have one without the other. This same maxim holds true for public schools. Most public schools have mission statements, complete with lofty language and a vision for what they would like to become.

Too frequently, we assume that we are meeting our stated mission and the values and principles that are an integral part of it. We go about our business strategically planning, collecting metrical data, and reporting the statistics to the public and media. We assume that by doing so we are developing credibility with the public and other sectors of our communities.

But integrity and credibility are more than a set of metrics. Along with the data we collect and report are critical intangibles—principles and values. The question is, Are we living up to our values and the principles that we espouse in our mission statement and operational procedures?

Accountability has two components. What we accomplish is obvious. Metrically measurable outcomes such as test scores, attendance and discipline records, fiscal statistics, and other data have been highlighted through standards and legislative mandates. Schools are also responsible, however, for how we work with children, parents, and the community to reach those tangible outcomes. In other words, does our behavior match our words and elicit trust, fairness, justice, and virtue? Are the values and principles inherent in creating positive, respectful, creative, nurturing, and compassionate relationships with students, parents, and others evident in our processes and behavior? Do we communicate clearly, without jargon and obfuscation, and do we listen to those we serve?

These questions cannot easily be determined through quantitative metrics. But organizations that do not have these intangible qualities and characteristics do not achieve a high degree of credibility and integrity. Metrics, achieved without a strong value base, can breach ethical and moral standards. The ends do not validate the means.

One approach to determining whether school districts have credibility and integrity and live their values and principles is through hosting an educational summit. Every two to three years, the district should hold an educational summit of a cross-section of the community to review quantitative and qualitative data about whether the school district's program performance, operations, and relationships match its values, principles, and mission.

THE PARTICIPANTS

A cross-section of the community is essential to the summit and should include representatives from the following: students (usually high school students who have been in the district for an extended period of time), teachers, support staff, parents, business, civic, and political leaders, private school representatives, and others who are important in your community. About seventy-five people will be a good cross-section for the community team.

To have credibility, this group must include representatives from all perspectives in the community. To eliminate critics of the school system and only include proponents of public education would be a mistake and would tarnish the integrity of the process. Integrity is integral to a summit from which the school board and administration can get unvarnished feedback and learn how the school system's performance and operation is viewed.

The role of the summit participants is to review mission and values statements, school district promotional materials, the goals of the curriculum and program, the metrical data and information about the performance of the school and its programs, the qualitative data collected through surveys, interviews, and other means about the school and its programs, state and federal accountability reports, and other information related to the district's mission, processes, and operation. The role of the board of education is to *listen* to the reaction of the cross-section of the community to the information about the schools' performance. Again, the board's role is simply to listen, ask clarifying questions of the participants, and solicit suggestions for improvement. The board does not make presentations or engage in debate.

The administration and the professional staff make presentations, provide information, and answer questions about administration, fiscal operations and expenditures, communications, personnel, curriculum, instruction, assessment, cocurricular activities, planning, facilities and grounds, and other processes and operations. The administration's role is to provide information, explain data, and answer questions.

A neutral facilitator is essential to the process. This person should be from outside the school system and have the process skills necessary to manage the meeting so that the school board and administration get clear feedback, conclusions, and suggestions from the summit participants.

THE PROCESS

Summits require at least one and a half days or, preferably, two days to be thoughtful and valid. The summit can be completed in a Friday evening and an all-day Saturday session. The facilitator is key to keeping on task and completing the objectives of the summit. A general outline for the agenda is:

Friday evening: presentation and review of the materials and operations

Saturday morning: presentations, questions, and responses to each segment of the school's operation

Saturday afternoon: preliminary conclusions and recommendations to the board of education

A major task of organizing a summit is to collect quantitative and qualitative information that accurately reflects all aspects of the school district's operations. The quantitative and qualitative data and information can then be reviewed, analyzed, and assessed against the principles, values, and goals of the school system by the citizens and other participants.

The key to collecting and analyzing this information is organizing it by the components to be reviewed, writing it in clear language, and providing backup information that might be necessary to answer questions. This information is usually in a binder and is given to the participants prior (at least a week) to the summit for their review. If done properly, the binder will be a very detailed accountability picture of the processes, relationships, and outcomes of the school system at the elementary, secondary, and district levels.

After the administration presents and explains the data in the binder to the seventy-five members of the summit, the participants ask questions, get clarity and understanding, and begin to draw conclusions. To be helpful to the school board and professional staff, the feedback from the summit participants must be focused and clear. Questions are helpful in this process. Questions that can be asked of the cross-section of the community include:

- Do you understand the information provided to you? Is the information provided to the community clear, understandable, and jargon free?
- Do our operational procedures and relationships match our stated values and principles?
- Do we provide the programs essential to meeting our stated goals and mission?
- Do our programs provide equal opportunity for all students to participate?
- Do our test scores and other metrics reflect the standards the community expects from its schools?

- Is the relationship of the board, administration, faculty and staff, and community healthy and positive?
- Do we provide adequate information to parents and others about the schools?
- Do you have confidence that the program and processes will produce the tangible and intangible results you expect?
- Are our procedures understandable and sound and reflect the valid values and principles we espouse?
- What programs, procedures, or materials do not make sense to you?
- In what areas do you think the district demonstrates strength?
- In what areas do you think it could be improved?
- Do you think the district has integrity; do our words match our performance?
- Does the district have credibility with the various segments of the community?
- Other questions (this list is not all-inclusive, and the staff can define questions this educational summit should answer).

The facilitator will work with the group to develop a presentation to the board and a summation of the conclusions and recommendations in writing. The results of this educational summit can be used in subsequent planning sessions, in providing feedback to the faculty and staff of each of the schools, and in reporting to the greater community the perspectives of this cross-section of the community.

The process of openly having an educational summit to review the school district in itself can build credibility if the information and the approach have integrity. The educational summit provides a greater degree of transparency in the operation of the schools and can lead to concrete suggestions and change based on the insight and input of the participants.

School Reform Strategy: Using Research to Reform Schools

Brenda Dietrich
Topeka, Kansas

I recently asked all staff members to reflect on whether our seven-hour instructional day makes the best possible use of time for learning. Four years ago, we implemented full-day kindergarten throughout the district in every building to give our youngest students the "gift of time." We have recently created uninterrupted longer blocks of time in our elementary buildings to devote more focused time to successfully meeting reading and math standards for students. The middle school has a math lab and reading lab for at-risk students, which functions as an additional block of time for learning our math and reading skills. The high school also has math labs and reading labs for students who need more time and assistance. These students are enrolled in a regular math class in addition to a math standards class or a regular language arts class plus a reading lab. At the elementary level, we have additional after-school learning time in math and reading in our computer labs using Success Maker software for at-risk students. The point of the question regarding how we use our seven-hour day was to remind staff of our focus on results for students and to use our time wisely to ensure all students learn at the highest levels.

Lezotte's (1991) research tells us that what gets measured gets done, and if you don't have the data, it's not happening. We have formed data teams in our district whose membership includes teacher leaders and administrators. Their charge is to carry the mission of data-driven decision making to the building level by analyzing and using data to improve teaching and learning. These teams meet quarterly and use the data derived from early warning assessments, DIBELS, state assessments, and grade-level common assessments created by teaching staff to make decisions about programs, interventions, curriculum, and assessment. Our staff members have been involved in identifying the mastery curriculum, which is aligned to the Kansas Assessment and is the top assessment priority in the district. To reach 100 percent of students at 100 percent mastery is our goal.

Our administrative team uses Lezotte's (1991) Correlates of Effective Schools as a framework for moving the school improvement process forward. Principals are trained to be instructional leaders. They support staff through the appraisal process, and every administrator, including myself, conducts regular walk-throughs to observe teaching and learning in classrooms. Our appraisal instrument was developed collaboratively with teachers and administrators and is unique in its levels of specificity to teaching skills, levels of performance, and standards.

Principals and teachers engage in book studies and professional growth opportunities to expand their knowledge of best practices.

Our staff models lifelong learning and is implementing professional learning communities in all buildings to increase our capacity for sustained improvement.

To be able to yield positive results in any district, the superintendent's primary job should be to focus all staff, both classified and certified, on the basic purposes of schooling. Jim Collins's (2001) study of great companies and organizations showed us that great leaders have unwavering resolve. Their beliefs permeate the organization through practices, policies, and, most often, plain old conversations. In Auburn-Washburn, every employee knows that his or her goal is to provide an optimal educational experience for all children, and everyone is responsible for the success of the district, from the bus drivers to the secretaries to the food service workers. We ask for their input and thank them for their service to our students. Our principals and teachers know that their job is to ensure that all children have the time and desire to learn the intended curriculum well. We have a collective mission, and we are all responsible for setting high expectations and applying a disciplined effort to make sure all students succeed in our schools. That mission is communicated to staff through our strategic plan, our practices, policies, priorities, and daily interactions. We believe that everything we do is a result of teamwork and our combined efforts as we work to make sure our students reach the highest levels of proficiency. We take great pleasure in our jobs and face challenges, such as NCLB, with a positive attitude and the belief that we can make a difference and that we have the responsibility to do so.

School Reform Strategy: Evaluate School Programs

Chuck Holt
Lexington, Texas

I believe as a superintendent that in-depth program evaluations should be made on at least a biannual basis. No program or department should miss being evaluated, and the results should be provided to the public. Although this evaluation process is not particularly unusual, I believe it important to report the findings to the board and community in a succinct and understandable manner. Besides the typical success evaluation model, I add extensive reviews including a cost analysis, comparisons to similar programs, and findings on efficiency and funding sources. The benefits of these formal reports are twofold. First, this type of reporting builds confidence in existing school programs and helps get new initiatives off the ground when needed. As an example, I recently reported to the board on a program review of our district's extracurricular program, including athletics and academics. Patrons were pleasantly surprised that our district spending for these programs is very small in comparison to the academic cost per student. Many were surprised that these costs were actually much smaller than even bus transportation or other segments of the school budget. These real-world reports help dispel misperceptions such as that all public schools spend undue amounts of money on athletic programs.

Second, the board and school patrons appreciate knowing that programs are actually reviewed in an objective manner. People understand that programs have a way of lingering after their usefulness or of becoming very inefficient. As an example, in a recent review of the district's custodial services, our report was able to provide cost-per-square-foot comparisons with other districts our size, make industry comparisons, and even deliver a cleanliness-level-to-cost ratio comparing other institutions with our school. This report allowed the board to fairly evaluate the cleanliness of buildings, program needs, and other relevant issues more accurately than when only hearing the incidental complaint.

Overcoming School Reform Barriers: Ask "What Doesn't Make Sense?"

George A. Goens
Litchfield, Connecticut

Most organizations become comfortable with routines, programs, and processes that have been in operation for years. Schools are no exception. Longevity alone stops or deters discussion of their vitality and viability. "We've always done it this way" becomes the obstructing mantra.

In making pragmatic change, asking a simple question can open discussion and highlight what people may have been thinking and harboring for years. "What processes, procedures, programs, or plans do not make sense?" You might be surprised at the results!

To get a different perspective on these questions, ask them of the following (do it in writing to be sure the person's anonymity is protected): central office staff and administrators, principals, support staff, custodial and maintenance staff, teachers at all levels, parents, school board members, town officials, community leaders, and other groups. Collect the feedback and begin to cross-check similarities, but do not forget the isolated comment—it may have great validity. The lone individual may respond with insight and accuracy.

Check all of the responses against the following questions:

- What processes, procedures, or programs are contrary to our values and mission or are obsolete?
- Can we operate more cost-effectively and efficiently without them or by revising them?
- Can we reduce bureaucracy if we eliminate or modify them?
- If we change or eliminate them, can we improve the work environment and climate and increase trust, effectiveness, and productivity?
- If we change or eliminate them, can we restructure work and utilize people's talents to a greater degree?
- Do any of them stymie people's motivation, creativity, and innovation?

The "what doesn't make sense" list can be used to start meaningful and pragmatic change that emanates from the people in the organization. The changes can have a practical impact on efficiency and effectiveness and create issues and topics for discussion.

You might be surprised at the positive changes possible by addressing those issues "that just don't make sense." Reform can start here, and better ideas can bubble up that people will support. This is one way to prune dead branches and unnecessary processes from the organizational tree.

Overcoming School Reform Barriers: Organizational Inertia

Robert Olsen
Sturgis, Michigan

In 1968 I took an undergraduate class as part of my major field of study. The title of the course was the Sociology of Organizations. It sounded a bit bland, and I really don't remember it as having any kind of profound impact on me at the time. Years later, however, after moving into a number of leadership positions, I found myself remembering that class as I sought understanding about how organizations worked and how I might best lead them through change.

What that class gave me was an early appreciation of the concept of organizational inertia—the idea that organizations spend most of their time and energy trying to replicate themselves while resisting virtually all efforts to change and reform. While I was taking the class, I could not have cared less about how organizations worked. But I do now! No matter what you call it—organizational inertia, maintaining the status quo, or resisting change—the reality is that, if you are attempting to drive a school district through the many reform initiatives out there, you simply can't do it by using your rearview mirror.

School districts are not alone when it comes to experiencing inertia. We hear about inertia all the time from key stakeholders of all kinds: parents, politicians, teachers, administrators, and pundits from all sides of the political and social spectrum. They all want to see schools change, improve, and "reform," as long as the school looks and feels pretty much the same way it did when they were in school! Ignoring the dramatically different reality our children now face, we are often stuck on the notion that, because we might have enjoyed a successful schooling experience, it stands to reason that more of the same is what our children need for success in today's world. And nothing could be further from the truth.

Another barrier to public school reform has to do with the inability of our key decision makers to come to any kind of agreement on basic content standards and appropriate instructional practice. Our inability to define and focus the necessary teaching and learning outcomes into a comprehensive and coherent national education policy is saddling future generations with a huge social debt. Our lack of agreement on what children should know and be able to do has a stunningly negative influence on reform efforts. The ugly impact of politics has crept inside the debate over those standards and practices, much to the detriment of positive school reform. Because of the polarizing force of current political ideology, we seem to have held hostage the best interests of our children, a sad commentary on our society, to say the least.

Many school districts prior to the latest reform movement energized by NCLB were fairly isolated. There were local curricula in place, an accountability piece in the form of some kind of mandated testing by most states, and of course adherence to local standards and expectations. In the past, pressure on superintendents had more to do with local issues than with statewide, national, or international comparative analysis. While many of us attempted to heighten awareness of academic competition from around the world, the vast majority of our constituency seemed most concerned with how we stacked up against the neighboring district on game night. Again, because of positive personal school experiences of the past, maintaining the status quo had become attractive.

The tide is rapidly changing. There is now a much greater expectation on the part of key stakeholders in my community for our district to do well in academic comparisons with similar schools across the state and around the world. People are excited, and the staff is much more focused and energized due to the intense scrutiny brought about by NCLB and Education YES! (the Michigan accreditation model). And although I still get the most questions about how the athletic team is doing, I find myself being engaged on a regular basis with questions about our latest test scores, the selection of our math curriculum, and the philosophy of our reading program.

In some ways, it has made my job easier, but mostly it's just different. I often seem to be navigating a mine field as I support and champion the federal and state mandates coming at us "fast and furious" while, at the same time, supporting our teachers by listening to their fears, complaints, and concerns as they address the requirements of reform initiatives. Regardless, the job continues to be challenging and demanding, yet immensely satisfying.

Overcoming School Reform Barriers: Three Suggestions

Brenda Dietrich
Topeka, Kansas

A committee of superintendents convened by the Kansas State Board of Education, in which I participated, identified many barriers or obstacles to change during working meetings with the commissioner of education. The "Kansas themes," which I believe are most likely universal in nature, centered on the need to move beyond the traditional school model; a desire for more long-range planning in all areas, including funding; the need for support for leadership development at all levels; and the requirement of equitable educational opportunities for all, regardless of demographics.

From a broader perspective, it seems to me there are three barriers at the heart of the impediments we face as superintendents when trying to extol the benefits of a particular reform to our board, staff, parents, and/or patrons. Overcoming these barriers has caused us to behave in new ways and required us to develop a depth of knowledge about the dynamics of change, aptly described in Michael Fullan's (2001) book *Leading in a Culture of Change.*

The first barrier that often impedes our progress seems so very simple but can be the key component to success or failure. This barrier, the need to *change the culture of the system,* I think we have the most difficulty with primarily because it is so painful to break from old habits and be expected to act in new ways. Jim Collins (2001) in *Good to Great* says that breaking this barrier requires pushing in a constant direction over an extended period of time. There are no easy shortcuts. The brutal facts regarding current culture and traditional structure must be examined, discussed, and abandoned, if necessary. Change is not something most teachers or administrators embrace willingly, but it can be done if we take the time to cultivate trusting relationships and agree on our purpose. Implementing reform initiatives requires a willingness to engage in selective abandonment. The challenge for staff members is to examine the internal environment of the school and determine, together, if what they are doing now is really working. We know that a critical factor in changing an organization begins with changing the conversation in the organization. We have to ask questions and construct solutions together, and we need to be able to find the time to engage in the dialog that allows us to explore those solutions. Time and perseverance are the most precious commodities when engaging in reform initiatives.

A second prevalent barrier to reform initiatives is maintaining the energy it takes to successfully *sustain the hard work of change.* As school district leaders, we need to provide pressure and support to create the conditions for success to ensure learning. If we are to improve the complex work of teaching, then our job is to keep on top of the change process, attend to the chaos that can result from change initiatives, and build coherence in the organization so that the momentum continues to build and grow.

Successful superintendents today need to be system thinkers and must have a commitment to a higher purpose. They must be passionate about every aspect of their job, especially that of educating students who must learn at higher levels rather than merely be taught at higher levels. It is our job, in this age of reform, to engage staff in a serious, professional dialog that focuses on continuous school improvement. You know you have succeeded if principals and teaching staff are as concerned about the success of other schools in the district as they are with their own. Maintaining this professional dialog has probably been the greatest challenge for me as a superintendent in this age of education reforms. I have had to school myself in the change process and respect the pain that staff members feel when they are asked to abandon the old ways or the traditional models and be pioneers who courageously explore those outposts of "best practices."

The last barrier to reform is one that seems insurmountable to districts who lack adequate funding: *we need increased resources.* There is a monetary cost to most reforms. We are all working on high school restructuring (as is most of the nation, I suspect), and there are many overt and covert costs tied to reform plans supported by current research. It seems reasonable to expect that there will be additional costs associated with staffing, materials, facilities, professional development, technology, and time as new reforms are explored and adopted. We expect to locate the resources required to not only implement the reform but sustain the reform. The challenge will continue to be, Which reforms do we embrace and which do we discard to allow us to move forward in the best interests of our students, preparing them for the skills they will need to be productive and responsible citizens?

Overcoming School Reform Barriers: Learn to Live With NCLB

Robert Olsen
Sturgis, Michigan

First and foremost, I believe the No Child Left Behind law had good intentions from the outset. It was intended to accelerate academic achievement for all students by putting a spotlight on the various subgroup populations identified in most schools. It was also intended to put schools on notice that accountability was finally more than a slogan used around election time. It was going to be the "real deal," with specific and significant consequences for poorly performing buildings and districts.

However, as it is with most major pieces of legislation, the intent of the law and the rules and regulations created to implement the law are not always in synch. As they say, "the devil is always in the detail!" The problem with the law as I see it is threefold. First, it was created using an ideological model that valued consequences in the form of hard-line punishment and sanctions meant to hurt and humiliate school districts, teachers, and school district leaders. Second, somehow those closest to the action—classroom teachers and building- and district-level administrators—were cut out of the design and development process. Decisions that had a direct effect on the way classrooms were being taught and buildings were being managed and led were made by people furthest from the action. Most of these decision makers had very little actual knowledge of life in the trenches or had been distanced from the real world of the classroom by either time or position. And third, decision makers and policy wonks seemed to have made an incredibly naive assumption that all children are somehow exactly the same, that they all can be expected to learn the same things, at the same time, and in the same way as everyone else.

Specific recommendations for living with NCLB:

1. If we really want to affect student achievement in this country, we must target preschool and early elementary programs with funding to support literacy-rich experiences for those children *and* their parents. I would recommend doubling the funding for programs targeting preschool, at-risk children.

2. The federal government must fully fund the initiatives that come with meeting the mandates of the NCLB law.

3. Identify reform initiatives and plan strategies using a national review board of current practitioners rather than a disproportionate number of bureaucrats, academics, and politicians with ideological agendas not in the best interest of the country.

4. Establish a nonpartisan commission that identifies the basic set of content standards for the nation in math, science, language arts, social studies (history, government, and economics), and technology education. Essentially, identify what students need to know and be able to do at the conclusion of

each course of study. Allow individual states to establish more stringent standards but also allow flexibility for schools to achieve results.

5. Maintain accountability for school performance and improvement. Set those performance goals for all districts in all states. Provide greater funding incentives for those school districts that are facing the greatest challenge and that show the most dramatic improvements. Require that the added funding be used on measurable professional development initiatives and enhanced instructional resources for students and teachers.

6. Based on previous performance on standardized state testing, target struggling schools and provide them with management teams, curriculum and instructional specialists, teacher and student mentors, and the necessary funding to retrain teachers and administrators before sanctions are imposed.

7. Maintain the focus on subgroup populations but identify realistic subgroup sizes consistent from state to state. Rules dictating testing and measurement of some special needs groups and limited English proficiency groups are currently unrealistic. Practitioners who work with those groups of students on a daily basis are best qualified to set those target standards.

8. Mandate changes to universities' schools of education programs to better prepare teacher candidates with exposure and experience with best practices.

9. Provide even greater incentives than current practice to college students who would pursue teaching degrees in hard-to-fill disciplines (industrial technology, mathematics, science, special education, foreign language).

10. Hiring and retraining highly qualified teachers is critical. However, to determine highly qualified status, the emphasis must be on more than the simple acquisition of content knowledge. It must be recognized that "highly qualified" has much more to do with good teaching practice than with acquiring content knowledge. Without that understanding built into the "rules," we are doing a gross disservice to our children.

SUMMARY

School Reform Research

Involve stakeholders in accomplishing shared vision in a collaborative environment, recognize leadership at every level, acknowledge that all are accountable for student achievement, establish a culture of inquiry, design authentic instruction, understand change, champion continued learning.

Best Practice Ideas for School Reform

- Align the curriculum
- Give early warning assessments
- Provide support for special populations
- Develop before- and after-school programs
- Address the culture of the whole school
- Host an educational summit to review district data, performance, values, and plans
- Provide professional growth through book studies
- Evaluate school programs regularly
- Cultivate relationships to support change
- Make NCLB work for your district

SCHOOL REFORM REFLECTION

1. What school reform efforts have been most effective in your district?

2. In what ways do your reform efforts emphasize infusing the district vision with a commitment to that vision?

3. What are you doing to help others in your district become better at implementing change?

4. Where are you weak in these areas?

5. Write a prescription for improvement for bringing about school reform to your district.

6. What ideas in this chapter were the most important for your school?

7. How can you implement or revise ideas in this chapter to improve your district?

ADDITIONAL RESOURCES

DIBELS test (The Dynamic Indicators of Basic Early Literacy Skills).
   http://dibels.uoregon.edu
Success Maker. http://www.pearsonschool.com/index.cfm?locator=PSZ1Aq
Waterford (software). http://www.softwarecentral.ie/Libraries/Waterford

CHAPTER SIX

More Creative Ideas That Work

The significant problems we face cannot be solved by the same level of thinking that created them.

—Albert Einstein

There is not complete agreement that a superintendent shortage exists today. However, in 2000, Glass suggested that fewer individuals appeared to be interested in becoming superintendents. At the same time, Cooper (2000) pointed out that 35 percent of superintendents who responded to his survey said they would not recommend the superintendency to other educators as a job choice. This leads us to ask two questions: What motivates people to seek and keep a superintendent job? and What are the barriers to seeking and keeping a superintendency?

Harris, Lowery, Hopson, and Marshall (2004) surveyed 25 percent (259) of the 1,036 Texas superintendents. Texas superintendents indicated that the three primary reasons they seek and keep the job are their desire to make a difference and positively affect people, the personal and professional challenge, and the ability to initiate change. One thirty-year veteran superintendent commented, "After a long day at work, I've done something good for someone" (p. 116). Superintendents participating in this study indicated that the four barriers to seeking and keeping the job were dealing with the bureaucracy, community politics, working with the school board, and the increased time commitment. As one superintendent wrote, "Most of the time, I feel like a conflict mediator, not a leader" (p. 117).

This chapter shares advice *for* superintendents *from* superintendents suggesting ways to navigate this difficult job for maximum benefit to others and to retain their original commitment to helping people. Pauline Hargrove provides practical advice for superintendents, and John Morton suggests ten strategies to help superintendents become more effective. Brenda Dietrich provides specific advice for new superintendents. She also reminds us of the importance of providing feedback. Robert Olsen in a snapshot comment challenges superintendents to do the right thing. Daniel King shares his experiences of moving from a small district to a much larger district. Tony J. Marchio shares advice for passing a bond, and Ronald D. Valenti gives very specific tips for a successful budget. Next, superintendents provide a recommended reading list for leaders. This chapter concludes with "Words of Wisdom" that superintendents often hear themselves saying to others.

Guidelines, Practices, and Words of Advice

Pauline Hargrove
Orange, Texas

BEGIN WITH YOURSELF

Be a person of character and integrity committed to doing what is right. Take time for regular reflection to analyze your means and methods as well as to assess your strengths and weaknesses. Build on your strengths and minimize your weaknesses for greater effectiveness. Exemplify excellence in all that you think, say, and do. Stay true to your values, and be willing to make the changes that will improve you and your service.

HIRE THE RIGHT PEOPLE

Consider only those applicants who demonstrate character, integrity, commitment to excellence, and a passion to inspire and enable success in others. Understand the magnitude, expectations, and potential effects of the position to be filled. Ask the right questions, create scenarios to be solved, review the portfolio and track record, and check credible references for each applicant. Make every attempt to ensure that the person to be hired likes to work with students and possesses the abilities, skills, expertise, desire for self-improvement, and caring attitude to meet the needs of the people they will serve and to accomplish the vision, mission, and goals of the district.

BUILD A TRUSTWORTHY, CARING, RESPECTABLE TEAM

No one does anything alone. Success takes teamwork built on mutual trust and respect.

Share a common vision, focus, and commitment to equity and excellence through collaboration and cooperation. Establish expectations and parameters, and then provide the individuals with the autonomy and resources to do the job. Remain accessible, and ensure progress and accountability through routine monitoring, assessing, and adjusting. Be willing to step aside and allow other people to excel in their areas of expertise. Spend your time doing what you do best and what others cannot do. The goal is to build leadership capacity, not to exalt one's self.

BE ACCOUNTABLE FOR PERSONNEL

Recognize that, in spite of their best efforts, sometimes people are not in the right profession or position to make the positive difference they are expected to make. Be sure to provide opportunities for additional training and development, mentoring and counseling assistance, and appropriate alternative resources as needed. However, if those efforts fail to produce the necessary results by the involved individuals, help them find another job or position that better suits them. Understand that "to carry them along" is not fair to the people they serve or to themselves and only leads to larger problems for all. Care enough to do what is right; release them from their assignment.

RECOGNIZE, PRAISE, AND CELEBRATE EFFORTS AND ACCOMPLISHMENTS

Provide recognition and celebrate the success of students and their families, faculty and staff members, the board of trustees, and the community at large. Send congratulatory notes; give pats on the back; praise individuals, teams, and schools publicly; share with the media continuously; and showcase excellence on the district Web site, in newsletters, and throughout the district and community, as appropriate.

Begin board meetings with special recognitions. When recognizing students, be sure to include their families and the appropriate staff. Thank families and staff for their dedication, cooperation, and support in enabling and empowering their students to be successful. Invite them to come forward so that the board members and superintendent can shake their hands to congratulate and appreciate them. Present the students with a special certificate of accomplishment. Take their pictures, add it to the district Web site, give them a copy, and send the information to the media. In the same manner, recognize community members and business owners who have made a significant contribution and provide them with a special certificate such as the Gold Star Award. Look for efforts by others to appreciate, and create awards to recognize them.

Send letters of appreciation to the faculty and staff as warranted throughout the year and, especially, during Teacher Appreciation Week. Provide a token of appreciation that is useful to the teacher and instills pride in the district, such as a leather portfolio, umbrella, or electronic memory stick with the district's logo. Always send a cake or some form of food along with the gift. Nourishment comes in different packages.

Provide a special convocation at the beginning of the year to welcome, inform, unite, motivate, and inspire the faculty and staff. In your superintendent presentation, introduce the theme for the year to create the focus, establish the expectations, and become a reference point for unity of purpose throughout the year. Showcase faculty and staff members as well as students, board members, and community members in the entertainment phase and in the presentation, as appropriate. Distribute tokens imprinted with the theme to everyone as they leave the auditorium through the drill team and cheerleader victory line and the playing of the district spirit song by the high school band.

End the year with a fun-filled recognition ceremony to celebrate service, success, the Teacher of the Year, and other awards and accomplishments. Remember, "The family that plays together, stays together," so immediately following the awards program, play baseball (if outside) or volleyball (if indoors). Enjoy visiting with your family members while eating popcorn, peanuts, and hot dogs.

Invite board members to the convocation, recognition celebration, and other school events. Recognize their presence and contributions so that others will also appreciate them. January is Board of Trustees Appreciation month, so make it special by providing a skit or some form of entertainment to honor them. Gifts of appreciation remind the trustees all year long that they are making a difference and that they are respected and appreciated for all they do. Finally, provide them with meaningful and fun experiences during their continuing hours of training as well as opportunities for fellowship.

Stay Committed to Doing the Right Things in the Right Ways at the Right Times

Because a superintendent serves so many different constituents—students and their families, faculty and staff, community, business, and industry—while being responsible for compliance with local, regional, state, and national requirements as well as laws, policies, and procedures, making the right decision can become quite difficult and uncomfortable. Seek input from the different stakeholders for a greater understanding of how issues will affect them; respect their opinions and viewpoints; collaborate with the board and administrative team; seek legal advice, if necessary; and then make decisions according to what is true and just. Recognize that decisions made for the group may not be what is best for the individual and vice versa. The right decision may not be the popular one or the one you want to make. Be courageous and make it anyway. After all, making the right decision is always the right thing to do.

Love the People and Enjoy What You Are Doing

You will be much more likely to be effective, make a greater difference, fulfill your purpose, and make others and yourself happy if you think, speak, and act in love. If you cannot love and enjoy the people you serve, consider pursuing another position for which you may be better suited. Life is precious; handle with care.

Advice for New Superintendents

Brenda Dietrich
Topeka, Kansas

My best advice for new superintendents is, first and foremost, to see to the details in your organization. It is easy to delegate. It's also easy to walk through a building and not connect with people. You have got to be aware of details. You have to ask questions all the time. Do not assume anything. I came to the realization many years ago that you have no idea what you don't know when you are new to a job or new to a district, especially when you are in a leadership position. I believe that, to be an effective superintendent, you have got to be aware of the underlying currents in your organization and of traditions, nuances, and people who are the informal leaders throughout the district.

My second piece of advice would be to work every day to build trust and a good working relationship with your staff and your board. A new superintendent should pay close attention to the dynamics of the organization and the traditions that are sacred. I always follow the advice of Lou Holtz, former coach of Notre Dame, who said in the documentary *Do the Right Thing* that to build a winning team you must

- treat people the way you want to be treated,
- always do the right thing, and
- don't try your best, *do* your best.

I ask my leadership team to follow these three rules and make them the guiding principles in their interactions with each other, their staff, their students, and their patrons.

John Morton's Top Ten List of General Advice

John Morton
Newton, Kansas

To steal a tool from the *David Letterman* show, here is my Top Ten list of general advice for superintendents:

10. Just when you think you've seen it all, it's time to remind yourself you haven't.

9. Being proactive and forthcoming with the media beats a surprise headline on page one any day!

8. Any issue can go from the ridiculous to the sublime (or the reverse) in an instant.

7. Some people don't want to be confused by the facts.

6. Never underestimate the power of the community grapevine.

5. It's great to have a daily schedule, but be prepared for the real events that will unfold spontaneously.

4. Always err on the side of the student.

3. Most people just need access to a listening ear.

2. Unfinished work will always be there the next day.

1. Every school year is a fresh start! Learn from the past to strengthen the future.

Feedback Is Important

Brenda Dietrich
Topeka, Kansas

Our mantra has become, "Feedback is our friend!" We need feedback whether we are a teacher, student, superintendent, or board member. It is an authentic and relevant form of evaluation that leads to critical conversations among staff and in the community if utilized appropriately and not dismissed as irrelevant. Feedback can be very painful for the insecure or the overly sensitive. It has taken us a considerable amount of time and some personal soul-searching to realize that, if what we are hearing is a criticism, we must not take it personally and become defensive but rather analyze it and learn from it. After all, the perceptions behind the feedback we are reluctant to hear and accept may not be accurate to us but are most certainly reality for the person who is the source of the feedback. We need to be unafraid to ask questions so that we can understand the feedback and put it in perspective. I wish more people would see the value of feedback.

I actually think you learn more from negative feedback than from positive feedback. The negative makes you look at yourself and reflect. Positive feedback is always welcome, but it is usually seen as an affirmation, which makes one feel good but may not be as useful. We provide opportunities for frequent feedback on programs, initiatives, interventions, policies, and so on and use that feedback as the catalyst for making changes integral to that never-ending cycle of continuous improvement. Feedback is our friend!

Another way we provide feedback and check for understanding is called "dipsticking." Our teachers dipstick regularly to evaluate what students know and are able to do prior to an end-of-the-unit test or quiz. Philosophically, this practice has been a shift from "I taught it, they didn't learn it," to "I taught it, some of them did not learn it well, so I need to reteach it." It is the marriage of Madeline Hunter's instructional model, which includes checking for understanding, and Larry Lezotte's *Correlates of Effective Schools,* which describe the value of frequent monitoring of student learning through assessment.

Doing the Right Thing . . .

Robert Olsen
Sturgis, Michigan

Somebody once told me that a great definition of common sense is simply doing the right thing, at the right time, and for the right reasons. If you can use that principle to guide your decision making, then things will work out—at least most of the time. It has proven to be a great piece of advice.

Moving From Leading a Small District to a Large District

Daniel King
Pharr, Texas

A couple of years ago, I moved from a district of approximately 3,300 students to a district of 30,000 students. When I interviewed for the job at the larger district, I was asked the question, How will you adjust from leading a small district to a district this size, and can you handle the adjustment? I said I thought it was a perfect match. I came up through the ranks in a small district where one has to wear many hats. As a small-district superintendent, I had to know the details; I had to meet with architects, know the construction, and know the budget. When I was assistant superintendent, I had a unique title—superintendent for finance and instruction. I oversaw the finance department *and* the curriculum department.

Prior to moving from a smaller district to my current larger district, I had been a finalist for a position at a larger district, and my youngest daughter was a senior in high school. She at first seemed willing to consider the move, but in the end she said she couldn't leave her senior year, so I pulled out of consideration. The point I am trying to make is that, when interviewing for that position, the board commented that I could talk about curriculum or about how many coats of wax to put on the floor because, in a small district, you don't have a team of administrators to turn to for those issues; instead, you get into the details about a lot of different things. In a small district, the numbers don't overwhelm you, and you have the opportunity to learn a lot. In a big district, you have a large administrative team, and people have areas of focused expertise. I'm certainly not going to claim to be an expert in every area, but I do know enough about all the areas to know what needs to be done or to know if things are getting done the way they should be. In other words, by coming from a small district to a large district, I have the advantage of knowing enough to supervise appropriately.

Administrators are normally curious individuals who learn by asking questions. In a large district, the challenge is in the logistics of managing all the numbers. If you become very good at that, then there would be an advantage when moving to a smaller district just in knowing how to really organize things. We can use our experiences, then, in going from small to large as well as when going from large to small.

Passing a Bond

Tony J. Marchio
Odessa, Delaware

One of the most effective strategies we have used in our district to pass a bond is to stay in the "bond mode" all year long. The bond mode for us means frequent written communications, town meetings, focus group meetings, and being readily accessible to all stakeholder groups. By operating in this mode continuously, we have been able to build trust with our community and support for our programs. I believe the public becomes skeptical when you communicate with them only when you want something in return. When we are not promoting a bond, we update the community on the progress of previously passed bonds, and we listen carefully to their concerns and ideas. The open communication not only builds trust but helps us wisely prepare a bond that effectively serves the community.

Collaboration Tips for a Successful Budget

Ronald D. Valenti
Rye Brook, New York

TIP 1: OBTAIN UNANIMOUS BOARD SUPPORT

Very few decisions, other than the possibility of adopting a school calendar (no joke!), are more crucial to the life and future of a school district than its annual school budget. Rather than a set of numbers to satisfy an accountant's appetite, the school budget lays out the educational plan for a district's vision, mission, and goals. It fashions the programs that strengthen student achievement and school performance.

The wise superintendent begins very early in the budget process to organize a framework for school board discussion and enrichment in this critical community decision. Board members need "buy-in" to three essential questions:

1. What new programs are being proposed, and what is their value-added contribution to student interests?

2. What are your best revenue and expenditure projections for next year compared to the actuals of the past two years and to the current estimate of this year's budget?

3. What will the proposed budget cost the taxpayer? What fiscal constraints and reduced expenditures does this budget include?

Both the board president and superintendent should collaborate on a timeline for school board member discussion of these essential questions, providing an opportunity for additional information that may be needed and for agreement on what role the school administration and staff will play in the public budget process. Some school boards also want to involve a citizen's budget advisory committee, whose members would be proposed by the board and whose purpose is to provide a third-party, neutral assessment of the budget's educational priorities and fiscal prudence.

Granted, this process is both time consuming and demands extensive work on the part of the superintendent of schools, but its value is incalculable. The necessity of forging a strong coalition of school board trustees, administration, staff, parents, and community members, particularly taxpayers who no longer have children in your schools, is the paramount challenge of the school superintendency.

It is the superintendent's leadership that will steer the ship's educational plan against the fierce winds of economic stress and taxpayer resistance. In the final analysis, the only good budget is a passed budget. If the community senses a divided board, oppositional forces will drive a tank through your proposed budget, and defeat is virtually assured. A united board and superintendent is the absolute first prerequisite for budget success.

TIP 2: HONOR THE BUDGET TRINITY

In building a sound budget that will withstand unexpected emergencies and unforeseen expenditures, superintendents must pay careful attention to the Budget Trinity of revenues, expenditures, and fund balances (Rainy Day Fund).

Let's assume a $30 million proposed budget and examine each of the budget targets in Table 1.

The cardinal rule for revenue assumptions is to budget conservatively. While the temptation is great to overestimate certain revenue lines to lower the tax rate or to permit additional expenditures, the day of reckoning for bloated revenue projections comes each year. A good rule of thumb is to underestimate revenue by 1 percent, which in our scenario from Table 1 gives you $300,000 in flexible spending if you propose a $30 million budget. Review both historical actuals and any changing circumstances before making your

Table 1   Tips for a Successful Budget (assume a $30 million budget)

Budget Target	Strategy	Flexibility
1. Revenue	1. Estimate conservatively by at least 1 percent	$300,000
2. Expenditures	2. Estimate liberally by at least 1.5 percent	$450,000
3. Fund balance	3. Maintain the legal limit suggested minimum of 2 percent	$600,000
TOTAL	**4.5 percent**	**$1,350,000**

NOTE: The New York State Legislature has passed legislation to permit the fund balance limit to rise to 4 percent by 2009.

revenue projections. They should withstand the dual litmus tests of reasonableness and fiscal prudence.

When the expenditure estimates are being calculated, the opposite rule applies. Estimate your expenditures somewhat liberally, by at least 1.5 percent. Again, in our $30 million budget, using this practice would provide an additional $450,000 to meet unexpected outlays or emergency expenditures.

Over the years, I've personally experienced crises ranging from excessive snow removal costs during a particularly stormy winter and the breakdown of the high school air-conditioning system to a major boiler replacement and the consequent environmental pollution of inlets and streams running through our schools. While all of these untoward incidents did not occur in one year, the point is that they did occur, and each stressed the budget for hundreds of thousands of dollars. Fortunately, conservative revenue estimates and flexible expenditure allocations absorbed these unanticipated expenses.

Finally, like any reasonable home budget, the school budget should ideally be expended at 98 percent of its gross estimate. In our $30 million example, that would leave a fiscal balance, unappropriated surplus, or Rainy Day Fund of at least $600,000, representing 2 percent of the gross budget.

Transparency is the key, and superintendents should educate their school boards and community to the necessity of maintaining

4.5 or 5 percent flexibility in the annual budget. During a good year, positive balances can, in part, be returned to the taxpayer in the subsequent year's budget as revenue, thereby keeping the tax rate down. In bad years, these funds will be allocated to address emergencies without taking crucial monies from the instructional program. Honor the Budget Trinity.

TIP 3: IN YOUR BUDGET CAMPAIGN, KNOW WHAT IS PERMISSIBLE AND KNOW YOUR NEGATIVE STRUCTURAL VOTE

Unlike political campaigns where candidates aggressively lobby for votes, superintendents are charged with educating the community about the merits of the school budget. But how far can the superintendent, central administration, and school board members go in educating the public? When does education become advocacy? When does advocacy become persuasion and, in some states, including New York, also become illegal?

New York's highest court, the Court of Appeals, ruled in 1986 that, while it is legally permissible for school officials to educate and inform the public about instructional programs and their financial impact on the school budget, officials cannot use public funds to convey approval of a particular budget or bond referendum, nor can they predict dire consequences for students and community if voters fail to support the budget. If, indeed, an appeal were successfully made to the State Education Department, the commissioner could, as a penalty, inflict his own version of consequences by overturning the election or removing school officials from office.

The best advice is to limit your budget workshops, coffees, brochures, videos, and PowerPoint presentations—all funded by taxpayer money—to simply informing the electorate with the plain facts of your budget. Of course, parent and teacher groups, using their private funds, can persuade and exhort the electorate (hopefully) to vote yes. But school officials are wise to stop at the water's edge of legally permissible promotion.

The Negative Structural Vote

As a school superintendent, I've organized well over thirty budget and bond referendum votes. There are obvious differences in the size and needs of a school district, the levy amount voters are asked to approve, and the tax rate they must pay to support budget and capital construction projects. But amid all these very real differences, there is one very real and stark similarity that, if used wisely by data-crunching superintendents, can be leveraged to our advantage.

The very real similarity is that, in every budget and bond vote, a certain number of voters will invariably vote "no" irrespective of how cost-effective your proposals or promising your programs may be. In fact, we have documented cases of voters, albeit small percentages, who have voted "no" even when your proposed tax rate is declining or the proposition calls for accepting state funds at no cost to the taxpayer.

This phenomenon, which I call the *"negative structural vote,"* argues that you can statistically estimate the number of negative votes that will be registered even before the budget vote is held. This information is crucial since a growing body of evidence suggests that time, money, and effort should be dedicated to encouraging supportive voters to come to the polls rather than attempting to convert negative voters from their oppositional stance.

Negative Structural Vote Case Study: Smithtown's Bond Referendum Vote

Table 2 outlines the actual votes registered when I was superintendent of Smithtown, a 10,000-pupil district in Suffolk County, New York. The June 15, 2000, bond referendum totaled over $140 million, with the main proposition addressing major renovations in all thirteen schools and an expansion from one to two high schools and from two to three middle schools. While we were quite confident Proposition 1 would pass, there was substantial concern that Proposition 2 would fare less well since that $13 million was to be used to build more kindergarten classes to provide for full-day kindergarten. In fact, the fear of defeat on that issue was so palpable we separated the propositions to ensure the major effort would not be stymied by the kindergarten initiative.

Table 2   June 15, 2000, Bond Referendum

Proposition	Amount	"Yes"	Percent	"No"	Percent
No. 1	$128 million	2,516	64	1,392	36
No. 2	$13 million	2,036	52	1,872	48

Prior to the critical June 15 vote, we analyzed carefully a five-year average of "no" votes between 1996 and 2000 and determined that we could anticipate approximately 2,036 "no" votes to each of our propositions. The budget campaign was thus designed to encourage at least 2,100 "yes" votes for each proposition.

1. Determine a realistic average of "no" votes per year. The five-year average during 1996–2000 was 2,036 "no" votes annually.

2. Determine the number of "yes" votes needed to pass the budget or bond referendum.

Without these statistical projections, we could have lost Proposition 2, and a very important early intervention program of full-day kindergarten would have been denied annually to 800 incoming kindergarteners for years to come.

Proposition 1 was so appealing the negative structural vote remained at 1,392 votes or only 36 percent of the total votes cast. But the resistance to Proposition 2 was nearly 500 votes greater, registering 48 percent of all those voting on that proposition. Fortunately, in both instances, we managed to encourage over 2,000 "yes" voters, and Smithtown has benefited from these positive votes ever since.

One small aside . . . on the night of the election, I asked each of my seven school board members how they voted on the propositions. While all seven voted "yes" on Proposition 1, three board members or 43 percent admitted voting "no" on the kindergarten Proposition 2. School board members should be reflective of their community's values, and these data demonstrate that assertion beyond a doubt.

In conclusion, stick to only educating and informing the public, let private groups spend their funds on lobbying for "yes" votes, and do the number crunching. Determine your negative structural vote, and mobilize sufficient "yes" voters to carry the budget and bond referenda.

TIP 4: MAKE SURE YOUR TAX RATE IS COMPETITIVE WITH YOUR NEIGHBORS AND SIMILAR DISTRICTS

Comparisons are odious! That said, literally everyone loves them— particularly taxpayers on budget vote day!

Superintendents within a region or particular geographic area are well advised to begin talking to each other early on about their anticipated budgets and tax levy increases. Barring exceptional surges in mandated costs, such as energy, health insurance, pension contributions, and so on, a handy formula for a reasonable budget increase is the combined percentage increase of the region's cost of living (COL) added to the percentage gain in enrollment. For example, a 2 percent enrollment rise for a school year when the COL is climbing at 3.5 percent certainly justifies a 5–6 percent budget increase.

A well-managed budget that maintains a healthy fund balance should generally keep the tax rate in a similar range, assuming state aid increases meet inflationary expectations and assessables remain stable or increase.

Tip 5: Remember, Public Funds Demand Conservative Stewardship!

In the final analysis, every dollar we collect and every dollar we spend is the public's dollar. We are the custodians of the taxpayers' investment in our children.

Beyond transparency and full disclosure in all expenditure transactions, the wise superintendent hires only the most competent business staff and personally ensures the integrity of financial affairs for the entire school community. Superintendents are well advised to spend the equivalent of a day per week or 20 percent of one's time reviewing budgetary allocations, proposed expenditures, and outstanding encumbrances. The superintendent should meet weekly with the business official and district treasurer to analyze cash flow, investment earnings, and any transfers necessary to balance individual codes and the entire budget. Numerous software programs are available to permit the superintendent to spot-check a broad range of transactions, thereby providing an added and necessary supervisory layer to the district's budget.

I've managed budgets as large as $250 million and as small as $38 million, and the lesson in each district is exactly the same—God is in the details! As superintendents, we must study and know the details of our school budget or suffer the unwelcome consequences.

BOOKS EVERY
SUPERINTENDENT SHOULD READ

Axelrod, A. (2000). *Elizabeth I, CEO: Strategic lessons from the woman who built an empire.* Upper Saddle River, NJ: Prentice Hall.

Blanchard, K., & Miller, M. (2004). *The secret: What great leaders know—and do.* San Francisco: Berrett-Koehler.

Blanchard, K., & Peale, N. V. (1988). *The power of ethical management.* New York: HarperCollins.

Bolman, L. G., & Deal, T. E. (2006). *The wizard and the warrior: Leading with passion and power.* San Francisco: Jossey-Bass.

Bridges, W. (2001). *The way of transition: Embracing life's most difficult moments.* New York: Perseus.

Collins, J. (2001). *Good to great: Why some companies make the leap—and others don't.* New York: HarperCollins.

Covey, S. R. (1992). *Principle-centered leadership.* New York: Fireside.

De Pree, M. (2004). *Leadership is an art.* New York: Doubleday.

DuFour, R., & Eaker, R. (1998). *Professional learning communities at work: Best practices for enhancing student achievement.* Bloomington, IN: Solution Tree.

Fisher, R., Ury, W., & Patton, B. (1991). *Getting to yes: Negotiating agreement without giving in* (2nd ed.). New York: Houghton Mifflin.

Friedman, T. L. (2007). *The world is flat: A brief history of the twenty-first century.* New York: Picador.

Gilbert, D. (2007). *Stumbling on happiness.* London: Vintage.

Glickman, C. D. (2003). *Holding sacred ground: Essays on leadership, courage, and endurance in our schools.* San Francisco: Jossey-Bass.

Goodwin, D. K. (2005). *Team of rivals: The political genius of Abraham.* New York: Simon & Schuster.

Harvard Business School Press. (2003). *Harvard business review on building personal and organizational resilience.* Boston: Author.

Heifetz, R. A. (1994). *Leadership without easy answers.* Cambridge, MA: The Belknap Press of Harvard University Press.

Jaworski, J. (1998). *Synchronicity. The inner path of leadership.* San Francisco: Berrett-Koehler.

Johnson, S. (1998). *Who moved my cheese?* New York: The Penguin Group USA.

Kidder, R. M. (1995). *How good people make tough choices.* New York: Morrow.

Kidder, R. M. (2003). *How good people make tough choices: Resolving the dilemmas of ethical living.* New York: First Quill.

Kotter, J. P. (1996). *Leading change.* Boston: Harvard Business School.

Lencioni, P. M. (1998). *The five temptations of a CEO: A leadership fable.* San Francisco: Jossey-Bass.

Marx, G. (2006). *Future-focused leadership: Preparing schools, students, and communities for tomorrow's realities.* Alexandria, VA: Association for Supervision & Curriculum Development (ASCD).

Marx, G. (2006). *Sixteen trends, their profound impact on our future: Their implications for students, education, communities, countries, and the whole society.* Alexandria, VA: Educational Research Service.

Marzano, R. J., Waters, T., & McNulty, B. A. (2005). *School leadership that works: From research to results.* Alexandria, VA: Association of Supervision, Curriculum and Development (ASCD).

Maxwell, J. C. (1993). *Developing the leader within you.* Nashville, TN: Thomas Nelson.

Maxwell, J. C. (1998). *The 21 irrefutable laws of leadership.* Nashville, TN: Thomas Nelson.

Miller, J. G. (2004). *QBQ! The question behind the question: Practicing personal accountability in work and in life.* New York: Putnam Adult.

Peters, T. (2003). *Re-imagine! Business excellence in a disruptive age.* London: Dorling Kindersley.

Pink, D. H. (2005). *A whole new mind: Moving from the information age to the conceptual age.* New York: Riverhead.

Pink, D. H. (2005). *A whole new mind: The rise of right-brain thinking and the new way to succeed.* New York: Riverhead.

Pink, D. H. (2006). *A whole new mind: Why right-brainers will rule the future.* New York: Riverhead.

Schlechty, P. C. (2005). *Creating great schools: Six critical systems at the heart of educational innovation.* San Francisco: Jossey-Bass.

Scott, S. (2002). *Fierce conversations: Achieving success in work and in life, one conversation at a time.* New York: Viking.

Senge, P. M., Scharmer, O. M., Jaworski, J., & Flowers, B. S. (2004). *Presence: Human purpose and the field of the future.* Cambridge, MA: The Society for Organizational Learning.

Senge, P. M., Scharmer, O. M., Jaworski, J., & Flowers, B. S. (2005). *Presence: An exploration of profound change in people, organizations, and society.* New York: Currency.

Sergiovanni, T. J. (1996). *Moral leadership: Getting to the heart of school improvement.* San Francisco: Jossey-Bass.

Sergiovanni, T. J. (2004). *Strengthening the heartbeat.* San Francisco: Jossey-Bass.

Wheatley, M. J. (2000). *Leadership and the new science: Discovering order in a chaotic world.* San Francisco: Berrett-Koehler.

WORDS OF WISDOM

In this section, I asked superintendents to share a phrase or phrases of wisdom that they often say—whether it originated with them or from someone else. I did not ask them to identify the source of their statement, but I'm sure you will recognize many of these powerful Words of Wisdom.

It's not why we can't, but how we can. Mark Keen

If it is to be, it is up to me. Tony J. Marchio

Seek first to understand before being understood (Steven Covey). Robert Olsen

Try to find win-win solutions—but when you can't be sure to win with humility, lose with dignity! Robert Olsen

How does that affect teaching and learning? Krista Parent

Is that best for kids? Krista Parent

The truth always lies in the middle, never at either extreme. John Morton

Work smarter . . . not harder. John Morton

Feedback is our friend. Brenda Dietrich

Do it with class or let it pass. Paul Kinder

Let's do it right the first time. Patrick Russo

There are no excuses for not thinking quality and excellence when it comes to the education of children. Patrick Russo

Leaders are more like poets than engineers. George A. Goens

The answer to successful schools will not be found in metrics. George A. Goens

Relationships are all there is to reality. George A. Goens

If you always do what you always did, you will always get what you always got. James L. Hager

Approach each situation with the attitude that "problems are solutions waiting to happen." Gary Johnson

First things first. Pauline Hargrove

Seek first to understand and then to be understood. Pauline Hargrove

Life is what you make it. Pauline Hargrove

Choose your battles wisely. Pauline Hargrove

Keep the main thing the main thing. Pauline Hargrove

Is this the best we can do? Pauline Hargrove

Attitude determines your altitude. Pauline Hargrove

The most important thing to remember is that the superintendent is all about building relationships. Diane E. Reed

It's not so much what you do. It's how you think about what you do that makes all the difference. Jerry L. Patterson

You live life forward, and you understand it backwards. Jerry L. Patterson

Adversity is a given. Resilience is an option. Jerry L. Patterson

We are more important than an organization; we can only be described an educational family. Chuck Holt

There is no such thing as status quo; we are in a state of constant change. The question is, are we getting better or worse? Robert E. Nicks

No excuses! Daniel King

If it doesn't get measured, it doesn't get done. Ronald D. Valenti

Always maintain a laser-like focus on school performance and student achievement. Ronald D. Valenti

The educational trinity for successful budgets and bonds: (1) high quality, (2) cost-effective schooling, (3) sensitivity to taxpayers' ability to pay. Ronald D. Valenti

There are two types of superintendents: those who are humble and those learning to become humble. Ronald D. Valenti

In the final analysis, we are all interims. Ronald D. Valenti

If you want loyalty, buy a dog. Ronald D. Valenti

Remember your personal mission, and never ever forget it when you are making tough professional decisions. Brian Knutson

What would you attempt to do if you knew you could not fail? Thomas Little

REFLECTION

1. What do you consider the most important reasons for seeking and keeping the superintendent job?

2. What do you consider the most important barriers to seeking and keeping the superintendent job?

3. Consider the advice given. What advice is most helpful to you?

4. What advice would you give to other superintendents? Create your Top Ten list.

5. Which of the recommended books have you read?

6. What Words of Wisdom do you find most helpful?

7. What Words of Wisdom do you hear yourself saying most often?

ADDITIONAL RESOURCES

Adaptive Schools. http://www.adaptiveschools.com

Cognitive Coaching. http://www.newhorizons.org/strategies/cognitive_coaching/front_cognitive.htm

Data-Driven Decision Making. http://rand.org/pubs/occasional_papers/RAND_OP170.pdf

Lou Holtz. *Do the Right Thing* [documentary]. http://www.beliefnet.com/story/198/story_19870_1.html

Mentoring Matters. http://www.mentoring-menasha.org

CHAPTER SEVEN

Superintendents Change the World of a Child

I long to accomplish a great and noble task, but it is my chief duty to accomplish small tasks as if they were great and noble.

—Helen Keller

The work of a superintendent is critical to students, and by being critical to students, the work of a superintendent is critical to the world. This is not just opinion; studies are affirming that there is a relationship between leadership at the district level and the level of student academic achievement (Waters & Marzano, 2006). As a young superintendent, when challenging problems occurred, I wondered how other superintendents might respond. Certainly every best practice of effective superintendents has not been addressed in this book, but this is at least a start.

When I analyzed the superintendents' responses about what they considered their most-effective practices, they confirmed the statement I made at the beginning of this book that *leadership is what transforms schools, builds community, acknowledges changing times, and implements appropriate school reform measures.* These components are all critical elements of the work of leaders who have a vision for increasing student achievement. In a variety of ways, participating superintendents shared their transformational leadership vision of improving student achievement by setting goals, they wrote of their commitment to nonnegotiable goals for achievement and instruction, they described collaborating and working with the board and other stakeholders, they consistently mentioned evaluating and monitoring achievement and instruction, and they noted the importance of passing bonds and developing partnerships to create resources that support the goals for achievement and instruction. In short, the ideas shared in this book are practical examples of leadership that affects student academic achievement. Waters and Marzano suggested that this effect could be so important that, if a superintendent improves leadership ability by one standard deviation, the average student achievement could potentially increase by 9.5 percentile points.

The transformational leaders who contributed to this book consistently talked about setting direction, redesigning the organization, and developing people. Leaders who built community began with the school board members, emphasized professional learning at the district and campus level, and were committed to strengthening relationships with the larger community. Award-winning superintendents acknowledged the changing times and addressed the new cultural needs of their students through programs and enriched curricula. School reform efforts were viewed through a lens that focused on student achievement. When giving general advice, these superintendents stressed creative ideas that resonated with principles of transformational leadership. These themes were not isolated to one specific chapter but were reiterated in other chapters as well.

As superintendents discussed their best practices, these three overarching leadership themes emerged

- **Setting direction** focuses on the belief that *student learning results in successful schools.*
- **Redesigning the organization** centers on the belief that *people are more important than programs.*
- **Developing people** focuses on the belief that *we is more important than me.*

Collectively, the target embedded in every submission was one of leadership that transforms—the opportunity and challenge given to superintendents to change a student's world.

STUDENT LEARNING
RESULTS IN SUCCESSFUL SCHOOLS

As superintendents set the direction for the school district, student learning results in successful schools. Ronald D. Valenti noted the importance of differential staffing to the school because this arrangement "best serves student's instructional and behavioral requirements." Patrick Russo brought together the whole community to shape a set of shared outcomes for community schools that led to growth in student performance. John Morton reached out to all schools in his community including private schools and home-schooled students in an effort to provide "support for all students." As Robert E. Nicks described how he developed cost-effective partnerships in his district, he pointed out that partnering works when it is "what is best for students."

Daniel King developed a school for dropout students designed "with students in mind." Pauline Hargrove led her school district by being the lead learner—in other words, her leadership role modeled student learning, with her own learning leading the way. As Michael McGill detailed how to prepare young people for a global community, he reminded us of the changing needs of today's students. He thus challenged educators to stay abreast of demographic changes and to engage students in new ways of learning through school curricula.

PEOPLE ARE MORE
IMPORTANT THAN PROGRAMS

When discussing the importance of leadership and redesigning the organization, Gary Johnson emphasized that leaders cannot have a plan for the campus or a school program without first having a "plan for your life." Chuck Holt addressed how educators in his district are closing the achievement gap with programs specific to the needs of the students. George A. Goens described an educational summit he holds where participants are brought together to evaluate school programs based on opportunities provided for all students. Mark Keen urged superintendents to build positive relationships with the media to publicize successes in the schools. By describing some of the communication efforts in his district, Paul Kinder reiterated the importance of communicating about people's needs to ensure "trust and a feeling of belonging" within the organization. Staying in "bond mode" all year helped Tony J. Marchio build organizational trust with people in his district. Thomas Little challenged superintendents to build community grounded in trust, communication, and positive relationships.

WE IS MORE IMPORTANT THAN ME

As superintendents wrote about their most-effective practices, they consistently talked of developing people in "our district" and of what "we did" or "are doing." For example, Robert Olsen noted that in his district "we know that the core mission of education . . . [is] to ensure that [students] learn." Thomas Leahy pointed out the importance of being a servant to others. Krista Parent shared the importance of continued learning together as a team and noted "our transformation" into a true learning community. Brian Knutson reiterated the importance of developing a professional learning community where everyone engages in continued learning. As James L. Hager described how he identified the culture of the district, he emphasized that this process led to developing strategic initiatives for the district where "we started together and the progression we had made."

In just one paragraph, Brenda Dietrich used the words "we" or "our" eight times as she discussed the achievement gap in her district and what their plans were to reduce that gap. In discussing the need for resiliency, Jerry L. Patterson and Diane E. Reed emphasized the importance of sustaining a strong support base because being a "Lone Ranger" rarely works over the long haul.

CHANGING A STUDENT'S WORLD

The culminating challenge consistently evident in all the submissions was that of positively changing a student's world. Nearly all superintendents started their careers as teachers. A few years ago, I taught a university class for beginning teachers. Each semester I asked my students why they wanted to become teachers. Most of them responded that they wanted to make the world a better place, and teaching young people was the way to do this. What a lofty goal! Today, I would argue that not only is this a lofty goal but a necessary one. Yet, as successful teachers are promoted to assistant principal, principal, and eventually to superintendent, it is easy for them to forget why they became educators in the first place.

So much is expected of a superintendent! The superintendent's job has become more complex, and so has the world. Because of this complexity, superintendents must remain focused on the needs of students. They must narrow their focus from changing the world to a focus on changing the student's world. Superintendents have lofty goals, and of course their desire is to accomplish great and noble tasks to make a better world for all of us—and certainly many do. But the reality is that their chief duty is to accomplish small tasks within their schools as if they were great and noble deeds. When superintendents lead with a transforming vision for student achievement in mind, their schools can change the world for a student. Only then can they begin to change the world.

The day is short and work is great. The reward is also great and the master praises. It is not incumbent on thee to complete the work but thou must not cease from it.

—The Talmud

References and Further Reading

American Association of School Administrators. (2000). *The study of the American school superintendency 2000.* Arlington, VA: Author.

American Association of School Administrators. (2008). *Leadership for change: National Superintendent of the Year Forum, 2007* [White paper]. Retrieved April 16, 2008, from http://aasa.org

Bennis, W., & Goldsmith, J. (1997). *Learning to lead: A workbook on becoming a leader* (Rev. ed.). Reading, MA: Perseus Books.

Blanchard, K., & Hodges, P. (2003). *The servant leader.* Nashville, TN: J. Countryman.

Blaydes, J. (2003). *The educator's book of quotes.* Thousand Oaks, CA: Corwin.

Brimley, J. V., & Garfield, R. R. (2008). *Financing education in a climate of change* (10th ed.). Boston: Pearson Allyn and Bacon.

Carter, G. R. (2003). Changes in educational practice. In W. A. Owings & L. Kapling (Eds.), *Best practices, best thinking* (pp. 247–253). Thousand Oaks, CA: Corwin.

Collins, J. (2001). *Good to great: Why some companies make the leap—and others don't.* New York: HarperCollins.

Cooper, B. (2000). Career crisis in the superintendency. In J. Natt (Ed.), *Superintendents see shortage of applicants for top spots as serious crisis.* Arlington, VA: American Association of School Administrators. Retrieved January 27, 2000, from http://www.aasa.org/In/Misc/01/27–00supcrisis.htm

Cooper, B. S., Fusarelli, L. D., & Carella, V. A. (2000). *Career crisis in the school superintendency?* Arlington, VA: American Association of School Administrators.

Covey, S. M. R. (2006). *The speed of trust: The one thing that changes everything.* New York: Free Press.

Covey, S. R. (1992). *Principle-centered leadership.* New York: Fireside.

Dahlkemper, L. (2005). Making the grade: School board members navigate education challenges. *SEDL Letter, 17*(2), 17–19.

Darling-Hammond, L. (2007). The flat earth and education: How America's commitment to equity will determine our future. *Educational Researcher, 36*(8), 318–334.

Davies, B. (2005). Introduction: The essentials of school leadership. In B. Davies (Ed.), *The essentials of leadership* (pp. 1–9). Thousand Oaks, CA: Corwin.

DuFour, R. (2004). What is a professional learning community? *Educational Leadership, 61*(8), 6–11.

DuFour, R., DuFour, R., Eaker, R., & Karhanek, G. (2004). *Whatever it takes: How professional learning communities respond when kids don't learn.* Bloomington, IN: National Educational Service.

Edmonson, S., Combs, J., & Harris, S. (2008). *Conflict resolution: 50 strategies.* Larchmont, NY: Eye on Education.

Elmore, R. (2000). *Building a new structure for schools.* The Albert Shanker Institute. Retrieved from http://www.ashankerinst.org/downloads/building.pdf

El Nasser, H., & Grant, L. (2005, June 9). Immigration causes age, race split. *USA Today*, p. 1A.

Fears, D. (2001, July 18). Schools' racial isolation growing. *The Washington Post*, p. A3.

Fisher, R., & Ury, W. (1987). Getting to yes. In W. M. Evan & S. Hilgartner (Eds.), *The arms race and nuclear war* (pp. 261–268). Englewood Cliffs, NJ: Prentice-Hall.

Fletcher, R. (2006). *Boy writers: Reclaiming their voices.* Portland, ME: Stenhouse Publishers.

Fullan, M. (2001). *Leading in a culture of change.* San Francisco: Jossey-Bass.

Gallagher, K. (2006). *Teaching adolescent writers.* Portland, ME: Stenhouse Publishers.

Glass, T. (2000, November 8). The shrinking applicant pool. *Education Week, 20*(10), 49–51.

Graham, S., & Perin, D. (2007). *Writing next: Effective strategies to improve writing of adolescents in middle and high schools—A report to Carnegie Corporation of New York.* Washington, DC: Alliance for Excellent Education.

Harris, A. (2005). Distributed leadership. In B. Davies (Ed.), *The essentials of school leadership* (pp. 160–172). Thousand Oaks, CA: Corwin.

Harris, S. (2004). *BRAVO—Principals: Building relationships with actions that value others.* Larchmont, NY: Eye on Education.

Harris, S. (2005a). *Best practices of award-winning elementary principals.* Thousand Oaks, CA: Corwin.

Harris, S. (2005b). *BRAVO teachers: Building relationships with actions that value others.* Larchmont, NY: Eye on Education.

Harris, S. (2005c). *Changing mindsets of educational leaders to improve schools: Voices of doctoral students.* Lanham, MD: Rowman & Littlefield Education.

Harris, S. (2006). *Best practices of award-winning secondary principals.* Thousand Oaks, CA: Corwin.

Harris, S., Lowery, S., Ballenger, J., & Hicks-Townes, F. (2004). *Winning women: Women leaders in education.* Lanham, MD: Scarecrow Education.

Harris, S., Lowery, S., Hopson, M., & Marshall, R. (2004). Superintendent perceptions of motivators and inhibitors for the superintendency. *Planning and Changing, 35*(1 & 2), 108–126.

Harris, S., Lowery-Moore, H., & Farrow, V. (2008). Extending transfer of learning theory to transformative learning theory: A model for promoting teacher leadership. *Theory Into Practice, 47*(4), 318–326.

Houston, P. D. (2006). The superintendent: Championing the deepest purposes of education. In P. Kelleher & R. Van Der Bogert (Eds.), *Voices for democracy: Struggles and celebrations of transformational leaders* (pp. 1–9). 105th Yearbook of the National Society for the Study of Education. Malden, MA: Blackwell Publishing.

Hoy, W. K., & Miskel, C. G. (2005). *Educational administration: Theory, research, and practice* (7th ed.). Boston: McGraw Hill.

Kelleher, P., & Van Der Bogert, R. (2006). The landscape of the superintendency: From despair to hope. In P. Kelleher & R. Van Der Bogert (Eds.), *Voices for democracy: Struggles and celebrations of transformational leaders* (pp. 10–28). 105th Yearbook of the National Society for the Study of Education. Malden, MA: Blackwell Publishing.

Lashway, L. (2002). *The superintendent in an age of accountability.* Washington, DC: Office of Educational Research and Improvement, U.S. Department of Education. Retrieved on October 28, 2004, from http://www.eric.uoregon.edu/publications/digests/digest161.html

Leithwood, K., & Jantzi, D. (2005). Transformational leadership. In B. Davies (Ed.), *The essentials of school leadership* (pp. 31–43). Thousand Oaks, CA: Corwin.

Lezotte, L. W. (1991). *Correlates of effective schools: The first and second generation.* Okemos, MI: Effective Schools Products, Ltd.

Lindsey, R. B., Roberts, L. M., & Campbell-Jones, F. (2005). *The culturally proficient school.* Thousand Oaks, CA: Corwin.

Lowery, S., & Harris, S. (2003). *Standards-based leadership: A case study book for the superintendency.* Lanham, MD: Scarecrow Education.

Lustberg, A. (2008). *How to Sell Yourself.* Franklin Lakes, NJ: Career Press, Inc.

Marzano, R. J., Pickering, D. J., & Pollock, J. E. (2001). *Classroom instruction that works: Research-based strategies for increasing student achievement*. Alexandria, VA: Association for Supervision and Curriculum Development.

Marzano, R. J., Waters, T., & McNulty, B. A. (2005). *School leadership that works: From research to results*. Alexandria, VA: Association for Supervision and Curriculum Development.

National Center for Education Statistics. (2005). *NAEP trends*. U.S. Department of Education, National Assessment of Educational Progress. Retrieved August 10, 2007, from http://nces.ed.gov

National Writing Project & Nagin, C. (2006). *Because writing matters: Improving student writing in our schools* (Rev. ed.). San Francisco: John Wiley & Sons.

Nelson, B., Economy, P., & Blanchard, K. (2003). *Managing for dummies* (2nd ed). Hoboken, NY: Wiley, John & Sons, Inc.

Olson, L. (2000, September 27). High poverty among young makes schools' jobs harder. *Education Week, 20*(4), 34–35.

Orfield, G. (2001). *Schools more separate: Consequences of a decade of resegregation*. Cambridge, MA: Harvard University Civil Rights Project.

Orfield, G., & Yun, J. T. (1999). *Resegregation in American schools*. Civil Rights Project Report. Cambridge, MA: Harvard University.

Patterson, J. (2000). *The anguish of leadership*. Arlington, VA: American Association of School Administrators.

Patterson, J., & Kelleher, P. (2005). *Resilient school leaders: Strategies for turning adversity into achievement*. Alexandria, VA: Association for Supervision.

Pawlas, G. E. (2005). *The administrator's guide to school-community relations*. Larchmont, NY: Eye on Education.

Price, T., & Harris, S. (2008). The role of superintendents in leading districts to cultural proficiency. In R. Papa, C. M. Achilles, & B. Alford (Eds.), *Leadership on the frontlines: Changes in preparation and practice* (pp. 236–243). The 2008 Yearbook of the National Council of Professors of Educational Administration. Lancaster, PA: DEStech Publications.

Reeves, D. B. (2004). Evaluating administrators. *Educational Leadership, 61*(7), 52–58.

Ruiz-de-Velasco, J., Fix, M., & Clewell, C. (2000). *Overlooked and underserved: Immigrant students in U.S. secondary schools*. Washington, DC: The Urban Institute.

Senge, P. (1990). *The fifth discipline: The art and practice of the learning organization*. New York: Doubleday-Currency.

Southworth, G. (2005). Learning-centered leadership. In B. Davies (Ed.), *The essentials of school leadership* (pp. 75–92). London: Paul Chapman Publishing and Corwin.

Suarez-Orozco, C., & Todorova, L. (Eds.). (2003). *The social worlds of immigrant youth. New Directions for Youth Development*, no. 100.

Tatum, A. (2006). Engaging African American males in reading. *Educational Leadership, 63*(5), 44–49.

Trotter, A. (2001, May 23). Census shows the changing face of U.S. households. *Education Week*, p. 5.

Waters, J. T., & Marzano, R. J. (2006). *School district leadership that works: The effect of superintendent leadership on student achievement: A working paper.* Denver, CO: Mid-continent Research for Education and Learning. Retrieved April 16, 2008, from http://www.mcrel.org

Zmuda, A., Kuklis, R., & Kline, E. (2004). *Transforming schools: Creating a culture of continuous improvement.* Alexandria, VA: Association for Supervision and Curriculum Development.

Index

CORWIN
A SAGE Company

The Corwin logo—a raven striding across an open book—represents the union of courage and learning. Corwin is committed to improving education for all learners by publishing books and other professional development resources for those serving the field of PreK–12 education. By providing practical, hands-on materials, Corwin continues to carry out the promise of its motto: **"Helping Educators Do Their Work Better."**

AMERICAN ASSOCIATION
OF SCHOOL ADMINISTRATORS

The American Association of School Administrators, founded in 1865, is the professional organization for more than 13,000 educational leaders across the United States. AASA's mission is to support and develop effective school system leaders who are dedicated to the highest quality public education for all children. For more information visit www.aasa.org.

CPSIA information can be obtained
at www.ICGtesting.com
Printed in the USA
JSHW010344010623
42499JS00004B/20